50
AIRCRAFT
that CHANGED
the WORLD

Ron Dick and Dan Patterson

The BOSTON
MILLS PRESS

A BOSTON MILLS PRESS BOOK

First printing in paperback, 2010

Library and Archives Canada Cataloguing in Publication

Dick, Ron, 1931-
50 aircraft that changed the world / Ron Dick and Dan Patterson.

Includes index.
ISBN-13: 978-1-55407-658-1 (pbk.) ISBN-10: 1-55407-658-7 (pbk.)

1. Airplanes--History. 2. Aeronautics--History.
3. Air pilots--Biography. I. Patterson, Dan, 1953- II. Title. III. Title: Fifty
aircraft that changed the world.

TL670.3.D525 2010   629.133'34   C2010-900298-9

Publisher Cataloging-in-Publication Data (U.S.)

Dick, Ron, 1931-
50 aircraft that changed the world / Ron Dick and Dan Patterson.
Boston Mills Press imprint.

[208] p. : ill (chiefly col.). ; cm.
Includes bibliographical references and index.

Summary: A selection of fifty of history's most influential aircraft,
with profiles of their pilots and designers.

ISBN-13: 978-1-55407-658-1 (pbk.) ISBN-10: 1-55407-658-7 (pbk.)

1. Airplanes—History. 2. Aeronautics—History. I. Fifty aircraft that changed
the world / Ron Dick. II. Patterson, Dan, 1953- III. Title.

629.133 dc22   TL670.3.D535 2010

Published by BOSTON MILLS PRESS
132 Main Street,
Erin, Ontario N0B 1T0
Tel 519-833-2407
Fax 519-833-2195

IN CANADA
Distributed by Firefly Books Ltd.
66 Leek Crescent
Richmond Hill, Ontario L4B 1H1

IN THE UNITED STATES
Distributed by Firefly Books (U.S.) Inc.
P.O. Box 1338, Ellicott Station
Buffalo, New York 14205

www.bostonmillspress.com

Design: PageWave Graphics Inc.

Printed in China

The publisher gratefully acknowledges the financial support for our
publishing program by the Government of Canada through the Canada Book Fund
as administered by the Department of Canadian Heritage.

Front Cover: *Aircraft restoration expert and warbird pilot Clive Denney flies a restored Spitfire Mark IX over the fields of southeast England.*
Front Cover Bottom Row, Left to Right: *The aircraft that trained the RAF, a de Havilland Tiger Moth, also flown by Clive Denney; the red Lockheed Vega flown across the Atlantic by Amelia Earhart, now at the National Air & Space Museum; the 1905 Wright Flyer III, on display at Carillon Historical Park, Dayton, Ohio; the de Havilland Mosquito, on exhibit at the National Museum of the USAF.*

Back Cover: *A USAF F-15E Strike Eagle taxis to the active runway at Nellis AFB, Nevada.*
Title Page: *Restored P-51 Mustang Li'l Margaret, flown by Butch Schroeder.*

Contents

Introduction

WHEN DAN PATTERSON AND I completed our five-volume *Aviation Century* series in 2006, we took some time to look back on the adventures we had experienced during the eight years it had taken us to compile the books. We had worked with museums and organizations in nine countries, written half a million words, created thousands of new color photographs, and searched for historic material in dozens of archives. It occurred to us that in the *Aviation Century* series we had built a firm foundation for other books on aviators and their machines. We recalled the people we had met and the aircraft that were their passion, and we began to think about those that had left the deepest impressions on our memories. It was a short step to considering a ranking system. Which aircraft deserved a place (together with their pilots and designers) in the top fifty of aviation's hall of fame?

Once the question had been posed, we soon found that a definitive answer was beyond our capabilities. We might just as well have tried to respond to "How long is a piece of string?" Nevertheless, we determined to make the attempt, realizing as we did so that any list of ours would be bound to leave out many aircraft that our readers would consider at least as deserving. What follows are our own ideas, arrived at after much discussion, soul-searching and fingernail biting.

The list begins, as it surely must, with the work of the Wright brothers. However, we chose to feature the 1905 Flyer rather than the machine made famous in 1903 on the sands near Kittyhawk. The first Flyer opened the door to manned flight, but only just. It was its 1905 successor that was the world's first practical aircraft. We then move to Europe and the dramatic events of World War I, recognizing the sad fact that aerial warfare is most often the spur that drives aeronautical advance. The interwar years are represented by a selection of trail-blazers and record-breakers, and by some of the aircraft that led the way in the development of commercial aviation. In the opinion of many, the era of the great flying boats was the last time that air travel offered elegance and luxury to rival the ocean liners.

Classic aircraft from World War II, such as the Messerschmitt Bf 109, Spitfire and Mustang, make up the center of the book, covering the astonishingly brief period that saw air forces move from biplanes into the jet age. They are followed by the competing jets from the Korean War, the MiG-15 and F-86 Sabre, and then by the F-4s and MiG-21s that saw action over Vietnam. In between come the commercial aircraft, the Boeings and their contemporaries, that created massive industries and changed the character of international travel. Burt Rutan's imaginative, mold-breaking designs are not forgotten. The last few places of the fifty go to some combat jets for the 21st century, such as the B-2 Spirit and the F-35, pointing to developments such as stealth technology, fly-by-wire controls and advanced avionics.

As we never tire of saying, in our opinion aviation changed the world more than anything else during the 20th century. We offer a very personal selection of the machines, and the people, that between them contributed more than most to that change, not only technologically, but also economically, militarily, sociologically and politically.

RON DICK
DECEMBER 3, 2006
FREDERICKSBURG, VIRGINIA

Photographer's Preface

LONG BEFORE WILBUR WRIGHT ever got off the ground, he wrote that "I have been afflicted with the belief that flight is possible to man. My disease has increased in severity and I feel it will soon cost me an increased amount of money if not my life." I have been infected with a fascination for flying for as long as I can remember. I grew up and still live in Dayton, Ohio, the home of the Wrights. There's still a lot of the kid inside of me, the one who will stop whatever he is doing and bolt for the door if even the hint of an aircraft engine can be heard. Often it's another airliner, or the local medical helicopter headed north on a mission. But every now and then it will be something special. The throaty sound of a radial engine may be a Waco biplane, the determined roar of a jet engine will be an F-15 leaving Wright-Patterson AFB.

The day in July of 1994 that Ron Dick called from Virginia to tell me that our bid to be the team to create the book that became *American Eagles; the 50th Anniversary History of the USAF* had been accepted, I heard the sound of very large reciprocating engines coming toward me. Fortunately I was on a cordless phone and, as usual, I headed out the door. It was obvious from the sound that this was not another skinny commuter airliner — this was an airplane that meant business. Through the trees that line our yard, I could just make out the large shape of a big airplane, now with four engines apparent. The last remaining flying B-29 Superfortress burst across the open skies and dominated my vision. Sleek, silver and huge. The bomber was low and climbing out from the Dayton airport, three miles to the North. Just like that, it was gone and the sound of the engines with it. A voice that I have come to know quite well came through the phone: "What was that?!" Oh, just a B-29, we get stuff like that through here all the time.

In retrospect I suppose it was a sign of great and wonderful things yet to come.

I have been able to make portraits of many aviators since then, and with that comes the chance to talk with these history-makers. I have found that we share a lot of interests in flight and the things that go along with it. One of them is model airplanes. Nearly to a person, as they grew up and honed their interest in aviation, they were building models of their favorite aircraft of the moment. Many of them still enjoy the process and the pride of making a model. Just like when they were kids.

When I started producing books about aviation, I thought, Hmm, wouldn't it be cool to make a model of all the different aircraft I have photographed. That was after the first or second book. Now, after more than 25 books and having photographed hundreds of different airplanes, I have given up on that goofy idea. But I still enjoy the craft and the challenge of making a good model. The photograph accompanying this piece is one I made just a few weeks ago, as I completed two or three that had been hanging around for a few years. I realized as I sat at my worktable that all of them are featured in this book. I have been able to cure my aviation affliction by becoming a part of it.

DAN PATTERSON
MARCH 24, 2007
DAYTON, OHIO

1905 Wright Flyer III

The First Practical Aeroplane

WILBUR AND ORVILLE WRIGHT were denied the benefits of a college education, but there was no doubt about their intelligence or inventive flair. They were methodical, self-sufficient and moderately successful. Their bicycle shop in Dayton, Ohio, gave them a solid background as light engineers and business-men. When they turned their attention to flying, they did so with predictable thoroughness.

Although the accumulated wisdom of earlier pioneers often provided a basis for the Wrights' work, they took nothing for granted. Calculations made by others were closely scrutinized and the figures corrected when found to be at variance with what had been achieved in the brothers' own trials. These systematic methods went hand-in-hand with a frugal practicality when it came to building a flying machine. The timber, fabric and wire they used were readily available in local stores, and they shaped spars, stitched seams, and rigged wings with their own hands. By the time they needed propulsive power, internal combustion engines had been developed to a point where their power-to-weight ratios made them just about suitable for aircraft. With their able assistant, Charlie Taylor, they designed and made an engine themselves and, since there was then no aeronautical propeller theory, they developed one. Starting from basic principles and building steadily toward their goal, the Wrights changed the world from the bench of a home workshop.

When the brothers built their first glider in 1900, it featured what the Wrights called "helical twisting of the wings," later described as "wing-warping." By altering the shape of the wings, twisting the trailing edge of one wing-tip up and the other down,

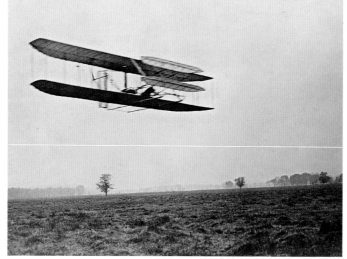

The 1905 Flyer airborne over Huffman Prairie. **Opposite:** The 1905 Flyer III was the world's first practical aeroplane. Full restoration of the Flyer was begun in 1947, under the supervision of Orville Wright himself. It is now on display at Wright Hall, Carillon Historical Park, Dayton, Ohio.

the brothers correctly interpreted the flight of soaring birds and overcame the problem of control in the rolling plane. However, they discovered that wing-warping introduced another problem. The wing that was warped down rose as it should, but it also swung back, inducing a sideslip toward the down-going wing. Vertical tail surfaces were added in an attempt to stop that happening.

By the end of 1902, the brothers were sure that they had a practical glider and they turned their attention to adding power. The water-cooled engine they built weighed about 200 pounds and produced 12 horsepower. It drove twin propellers via a system of simple bicycle-style chains and sprockets. If the engine was a triumph of do-it-yourself light engineering, the propellers were works of art. They were 8 feet across and shaped with a gentle twist. In the absence of information on propellers other than marine, the brothers determined their form by viewing them as wings moving through the air along a helical path in the vertical plane. The concept was difficult, but the finished propellers proved to be remarkably efficient.

The first Wright Flyer was built in the summer of 1903 and taken to Kill Devil Hill, near Kitty Hawk on North Carolina's Outer Banks. By the time preparations were complete, it was winter. On the morning of December 17, there was a cutting northerly breeze averaging 25 miles per hour, almost too strong, but the brothers agreed that they should try to fly. At about 10:35 A.M., with Orville aboard, the machine moved forward along its launching rail, with Wilbur running alongside steadying a wing-tip. After traveling for some 40 feet, the Flyer rose into the air. In a mere twelve seconds of undulating progress, the door opened on the

At Carillon Historical Park, a nattily dressed figure of Orville lies prone in the hip cradle and grasps the controls of the Flyer III, awaiting flight.

aviation century. By the end of the day, the door was much further open. Alternating as pilot, the brothers made four flights. On the last, Wilbur remained airborne for 59 seconds and traveled 852 feet. Given the strength of the wind, the actual distance through the air was about half a mile.

The Flyer's place in aviation history is assured, but it never flew again. The career of one of the world's most famous aeroplanes was over after it had flown for a total of little more than a minute and a half. The significance of the achievement was nonetheless immense, yet it passed almost unnoticed. To most people it seemed unlikely that an obscure pair of bicycle mechanics would succeed [where] others had failed. The claims of the Wrights were [v]iewed with great scepticism.

[Pub]lic interest had little effect on the Wrights. [T]heir first Flyer was an unsatisfactory flying [...] [s]et out to make it better. By the spring of 1904, [...] [re]ady. Similar to its predecessor, it was sturdier [... po]wer engine. Now engaged in powered flying, [... they] needed the fresh breezes of the Outer [...] [shif]ted their trials from an 80-acre field near Dayton known as Huffman Prairie. To make up for the relative lack of wind in Ohio, they erected a derrick and hung 600 pounds of metal weights from a rope inside it. The rope ran from the top of the derrick, under the launching rail, to the front of the Flyer II's trolley. When ready, the pilot tripped a catch restraining the weights and the aircraft surged forward to takeoff.

During 1904, the brothers made over 100 flights in the Flyer II. None was very long but a great deal was learned. In 1905, the Wrights poured their experience into designing a third aeroplane. In its final form, the Flyer III was a more aesthetically pleasing and effective machine than either of its forebears. The front and rear control surfaces were mounted further from the wings, producing an aircraft that was both graceful and maneuverable. By the end of the year, Flyer III had proved capable of completing tight figure-of-eight patterns and flying for as long as its fuel lasted, which on October 5 was for more than 38 minutes. It was the world's first practical flying machine. All this was accomplished at a time when no other would-be aviator had achieved any kind of controlled powered flight, and when most people refused to accept that such a thing was possible.

Left: A century after the Wright brothers flew their Flyer III over Huffman Prairie, Mark Dussenberry of Dover, Ohio, completed his construction of an exact replica of the world's first practical aeroplane. Here he stands appropriately dressed on Huffman Prairie, with his Flyer and the aircraft's launching pylon in the background. Huffman Prairie survives in almost original condition as part of the Dayton Aviation Heritage National Historical Park. It lies within the boundaries of Wright-Patterson Air Force Base, home of the U.S. Air Force Research Laboratory.

Below: Given the necessary impetus by weights falling within the pylon, the Flyer left its launching rail on October 5, 2005, and was flown gracefully by Mark over the same ground traversed by the Wright's flying machine exactly 100 years earlier. On that day, October 5, in 1905, Wilbur flew 24 miles in 39.5 minutes. It was apparent that Mark had mastered the hip movement required by the Wright's wing-warping control system. The few thousand people who witnessed the flight counted themselves fortunate to be on hand for this eminently successful recreation of a great achievement in aviation history.

Louis Blériot and his Type XI

Closing the Gap

IT WAS 1907 BEFORE FRENCHMEN began to make a real impact on the flying world, the most important advances being made initially by Louis Blériot and the Voisin brothers. Blériot spent the year building, flying and crashing a number of designs, impatiently abandoning each in turn without benefit of testing and modification, but in the process establishing through trial and error the classic monoplane configuration, with the engine and propeller in the nose, the wings well forward, and a long fuselage ending in a tail unit, the whole resting on an undercarriage of two main wheels and a tail-wheel.

By 1909 the heavier-than-air flying machine was beginning to gain some public acceptance as a practical airborne vehicle. Biplanes remained the dominant form, but monoplanes gained some prominence. Blériot produced his *Type XI*, the latest of his fragile line, and determined that he would use it to fly across the English Channel. The London *Daily Mail* newspaper offered a prize of £1,000 as encouragement to whoever was first to complete the flight between France and England. The dashingly handsome figure of Hubert Latham was first away in his *Antoinette IV*. Powered by a 50-horsepower engine, its long slim fuselage was reminiscent of a canoe, which proved fortunate. As he was born of French and English parents, it seemed entirely appropriate that Latham should be the one to complete the aerial bridge. He took off full of confidence from Sangatte, near Calais, on July 19, only to have his engine fail in mid-Channel. His aircraft's boat shape and its broad wings kept him afloat until he could be rescued by the French navy. Latham remained nonchalant throughout. As he described it: "I settled on the water in a horizontal position.

Fighting to keep his frail aircraft from falling into the English Channel, Louis Blériot makes for Dover on July 25, 1909. **Opposite:** Old Warden airfield, near Bedford, England, is home to the Shuttleworth Collection. Among their treasures is a Blériot Type XI, the world's oldest aeroplane/engine combination still in flying condition. One of the original machines flown at Hendon, it crashed in 1912 and was stored under Blackfriars Railway Bridge in London for years.

I swung my feet up on to a cross-bar to prevent them getting wet. Then I took out my cigarette case, lit a cigarette, and waited."

Latham determined to repeat the attempt and had *Antoinette VII* made ready at Sangatte. Meanwhile, not far away at Les Baraques, Blériot was ready to go with his tiny *Type XI*. The weather intervened, however, and strong winds kept both airmen grounded for several days. Finally, in the early hours of July 25, Blériot, awake because of a troublesome burn on his foot suffered in an accident a few days before, noticed that the wind had dropped. At 3:30 A.M., he air-tested the *Type XI*. Satisfied that all was well, he refueled and took off at 4:41 A.M., heading out into a mist over the grey waters of the Channel. Ten minutes later, without a compass or a watch, and with the 25-horsepower Anzani engine already showing signs of overheating, Blériot had outpaced the escorting French destroyer. In a later account, he said: "For ten minutes I was on my own, isolated, lost in the middle of the foaming sea, seeing no point on the horizon, perceiving no boat." He flew between 150 and 300 feet above the sea and "let the aeroplane take its own course. Then, twenty minutes after I have left the French coast, I see the cliffs of Dover, the castle, and away to the west the spot where I had intended to land…. It is evident that the wind has taken me out of my course." It had indeed, and Blériot had further difficulties when he tried to reach his planned landing place. The freshening wind threatened to prevent him from crossing the cliffs, but he managed to coax the *Type XI* through a gap and make a rough landing near Dover Castle. With a flight of a little less than 37 minutes, Louis Blériot had won the *Daily Mail*'s prize and written his name large on the

The Blériot XI's open fuselage contributed to stability more than if it had been covered, owing to the significant drag it created. Construction was of ash, bamboo and metal tubing, reinforced with piano wire. The back of the pilot's wooden seat can be seen in the foreground, with the exposed fuel tank placed further forward in the fuselage, behind the Anzani engine.

pages of aviation history. People everywhere began to give some thought to the proposition that the aeroplane could be much more than a mere sportsman's plaything.

British commentators were among the first to register some concern. As H.G. Wells said: "In spite of our fleet, this is no longer, from the military point of view, an inaccessible island." Alan Cobham agreed: "In matters of defence, we live on an island no longer. The day that Blériot flew the Channel marked the end of our insular safety, and the beginning of a time when Britain must seek another form of defence beside ships." Although the frail little *Type XI* could hardly be seen as endangering national security, it would not be long before events showed the potential airborne threat to be very real.

By 1911, European aircraft designs led the aviation world, notably Blériot monoplanes. If anything served to illustrate the lead French aircraft designers held at this stage, it was the fact that so many of their designs were being built under licence in the United States. Blériots were sold complete for $1,000, carrying the proud boast: "All assembled machines guaranteed to fly!"

They were used successfully to set records, win races and blaze trails. One triumph ended in tragedy when the Peruvian Georges Chavez succeeded in crossing the Alps in a Blériot via the Simplon Pass at nearly 7,000 feet only to be killed on landing at Domodossola in Italy. Elsewhere in Europe, there were long-distance races, including two 1,000-mile circuits, one from Paris, which circled via Brussels and London, and the other, an event again sponsored by the *Daily Mail*, round Britain. Both were won by André Conneau (pseudonym Beaumont) flying a Blériot. Recording his experiences in a book that became a bestseller, *Mes Trois Grandes Courses*, Conneau stressed the feeling of liberation and the invigorating challenge he found while flying his little monoplane: "[The aviator] follows a path free of any limitation. At his pleasure, he can ascend, descend, maneuver; he meets no obstacle. He is truly free … the victorious machine that he has created obeys his every movement with the lightness of a bird. The danger? But danger is one of the attractions of flight. If man loves flying so much, it is because every leap forward he makes toward the conquest of space threatens his existence."

Right: Blériot XI2 "PEGOUD" is displayed at Le Bourget inverted for good reason. Adolphe Pégoud was the most celebrated pre-WWI aerobatic pilot. He was the second pilot to complete a loop (the Russian Nesterov was the first) and the first to abandon a single-seat aeroplane by parachute. The Type XI proved popular both with serious competitors such as Pégoud and amateur fliers. In 1910, a Blériot XI would have cost a private buyer over $1,000, engine included. **Below:** The Blériot's wide steel frame had the dual purpose of carrying the wide castoring undercarriage and providing a firm mounting for the engine. Because the wheels castored, the machine could, theoretically, have been landed in a strong crosswind. Dan Patterson's photograph emphasizes the elegance of early aircraft construction. Light streams through the translucent fabric, revealing curving spars, while gleaming metal shapes fill out the fragile fuselage, and taut wires brace the aircraft for flight.

Fokker E.III

Boelcke, Immelman and the Eindecker

THE FIRST SERIOUS ATTEMPTS to develop a method of achieving air superiority in World War I were made by the French. Toward the end of 1914, the celebrated aviator Roland Garros revived the work done before the war by Raymond Saulnier on a system for firing a machine gun through the propeller. He had steel deflector plates fitted to the propeller of his Morane-Saulnier Parasol monoplane and a Hotchkiss machine gun mounted on the fuselage in front of the cockpit. On April 1, 1915, he intercepted a formation of Albatros two-seaters and shot one down in flames. The remaining Germans fled to report on the terrifying phenomenon of a single-seat aircraft that could fire a machine gun straight forward. Garros shot down a second German aircraft on April 15 and a third three days later. Flying again on the day of his third victory, Garros had his aircraft damaged by ground fire and was forced to land near Courtrai. A single rifle bullet had severed a fuel line and delivered the secret of the French success to the Germans.

Given the task of producing a similar system, the young Dutch engineer Anthony Fokker went one better. Within five weeks, his team produced an engine-driven cam mechanism that stopped a gun firing whenever a propeller blade was in front of the muzzle. By July 1915, Fokker E.III monoplanes (Eindeckers) were flying with synchronizing gear fitted, and the period of the air war known to the Allies as the "Fokker Scourge" began. In retrospect, it seems extraordinary that such a limited aircraft should have become the first real fighter and remain dominant for as long as it did. The Eindecker was an unremarkable performer even for its day. Its maximum speed was 87 miles per hour and it took over

Henri Farre's painting of a Breguet-Michelin bomber pursued by a Fokker Eindecker shows that French aircrews sometimes had to resort to desperate measures to defend themselves from the Fokker scourge. Note the crewman armed with a rifle lying on the wing. **Opposite:** From the Museum of Flight's archives in Seattle, a period image of an Eindecker, the first true fighter.

half an hour to climb to 10,000 feet. Control was still exercised by wing-warping and it was not easy to fly. After several fatal accidents, the Fokker training unit was disbanded and production was slowed so that only 86 Eindeckers were produced in 1915. The German authorities thereby unwittingly limited the Eindecker's impact on the air war, a fact which in 1915 must have been less than obvious to the Allies, who saw only that their losses were mounting alarmingly. Imperfect though it was, in the hands of pilots such as Max Immelman and Oswald Boelcke, the Fokker E.III gave the Germans a decided edge in the air.

Boelcke could see the possibilities offered by the Fokker E.III and he set about developing a system of fighter tactics. He emphasized the advantages of superior height and of being into sun. Two-seaters were to be attacked from below and behind, and all attacks were to be pressed in to close range before opening fire. Fighters operating in pairs should cover each other. When attacked themselves, pilots should turn into the attack, making the enemy's shot as difficult as possible. Boelcke also recommended the establishment of specialized pursuit units, rather than placing pairs of fighters in squadrons with mixed responsibilities. Max Immelman added the benefits of vertical maneuvering, giving his name to the "Immelman turn," a half-loop or steep climbing turn with a roll-out at the top. Boelcke and Immelman flew Eindeckers together to prove these tactics and were eminently successful. Both officers were awarded the coveted *Pour le Merite* (Blue Max) for their exploits. Immelman shot down 15 Allied aircraft before himself falling on June 15, 1916, during a combat with FE2bs of 25

Squadron, RFC. Boelcke survived until October 28, 1916, when he was killed in an Albatros scout after colliding with a wingman, Erwin Bohme, during an attack on British reconnaissance aircraft. His score of victories had risen to 40. In a manual written in 1916, he established principles for aerial combat that formed the basis for fighter tactics adopted by air forces everywhere. His ideas have stood the test of time and remain essentially sound as military aviation enters the 21st century.

In the absence of a synchronizing system to match that of the Eindeckers, both the French and the British tried other ways of countering the threat. On January 14, 1916, the RFC issued an order establishing reconnaissance policy: "Until the Royal Flying Corps are in possession of a machine as good as or better than the German Fokker… it must be laid down as a hard and fast rule that a machine proceeding on reconnaissance must be escorted by at least three other fighting machines. These machines must fly in close formation and a reconnaissance should not be continued if any of the machines becomes detached…. Flying in close formation must be practised by all pilots."

Effective escorts were not available, so this meant that a number of two-seaters had to fly together, offering covering fire as best they could. Close formation flying soon became common practice. It was noticed that Eindeckers tended to shy away from large formations, fearing the potentially formidable barrage of defensive fire, but this beneficial effect had a downside. Assigning multiple aircraft to each task effectively cut the available Allied front-line strength and reduced the number of reconnaissance sorties possible. This in turn led to insistent calls from commanders for more squadrons, increasing the demands placed on the training system and on aircraft industries struggling to develop while competing for materials with every other facet of the war effort.

Limited in performance it may have been, but the Fokker E.III made its mark on aviation history as the first effective fighter, forcing the Allies to change operational tactics and scramble to produce an effective countermeasure. Not until the introduction in January 1916 of the Nieuport 11 Bébé, which had a machine gun mounted on the top wing firing over the propeller, could the Allies begin to redress the balance of the air war.

The first E.III Eindeckers appeared on the western front in August 1915. While not impressive performers, they did prove dominant in the air. The interrupter gear designed by Fokker was an innovation that allowed the pilot to fire his machine gun through the propeller.

Proud E.III crewmen and the squadron mascot pose for the camera. Oswald Boelcke, who established basic principles and devised a sysem of tactics for aerial combat, earned 40 aerial victories, many while flying the Fokker E.III Eindecker.

Caproni Ca.3

Strategic Bombing Begins

WAR ON THE SOUTHWESTERN front of the Central Powers in Europe broke out in May 1915, with Italy's declaration of war against Austria-Hungary. The Italian Aeronautica del Regio Esercito (Royal Army Air Service) was not well prepared for the conflict, equipped as it mostly was with obsolescent aircraft, mainly Nieuports, Maurice Farmans and Bleriots. On the positive side, the Italians were the only country to have an aircraft designed from the outset as a big bomber. The pioneer Italian aircraft constructor Gianni Caproni had flown his first trimotor biplane, the Ca.30, in 1913. This led to a production bomber, the Ca.32, early examples of which reached frontline squadrons in mid-1915 and began operations on August 20, when they raided the Austro-Hungarian airfield at Aisovizza.

A curious bureaucratic drama lay behind the acquisition of the Capronis. Giulio Douhet, one of air power's prophets, was commander of the Italian aviation battalion in 1914. Convinced of the potential benefits of the aircraft as a strategic weapon, he used his initiative and personally authorized Caproni to build his bomber. Admirable though the Ca.32 proved to be,

A pioneer of strategic bombing, Gianni Caproni designed and flew a large multi-engined aircraft less than ten years after the Wrights first flew. Here he is with an Italian officer in the second production Ca.300. **Opposite:** A well-restored example of a Ca.36 is among the exhibits at the National Museum of the USAF. In the open cockpit of the boat-shaped nose, two pilots and a gunner are crammed together. The gunner manned a single 7.7 mm Revelli machine gun.

Douhet's superiors removed him from his post to discipline him for exceeding his authority. Refusing to fade away, Douhet continued to promote his doctrine, sowing the seeds of strategic air power where he could. In 1916, he was jailed for a while after he left a paper critical of Italian war policies on a train. Undeterred, he wrote and published essays from his prison cell agitating for an Allied fleet of strategic bombers. In "The Great Aerial Offensive," he urged Italy to build 1,000 bombers, France 3,000, Britain 4,000 and the United States 12,000. Released from prison in October 1917, he returned to military aviation, but not until after the war were Douhet's contributions to air power reexamined and his intellectual respectability restored.

After the first long-distance raid in August 1915, the Italians used their big Capronis to good effect, blunting Austrian ground offensives and attacking more distant targets. The strategic bombing missions were extremely challenging, especially those that crossed the Alps in midwinter to strike targets in Austria. Besides facing the threat of enemy fighters, the crews navigated through mountainous territory in all weather, often operating their heavily loaded bombers at heights close to their ceilings to avoid Alpine peaks. They were exposed to the chilling below-zero slipstream for hours in open cockpits, the rear gunner especially unprotected on his railed platform above the central engine. In pursuing their campaign with such resolution, they showed that long-range bombing was a practical proposition and bolstered the theories of strategists such as Douhet, whose persistent presentation of the case for strategic air power helped to shape the postwar development of military aviation.

Caproni bombers introduced Americans to strategic bombing. An agreement was reached between the United States and Italy for American airmen to be trained to fly the Capronis at Foggia. Managing the program was a U.S. congressman who had volunteered for the Air Service — Fiorello LaGuardia, later mayor of New York. As an Italian-speaking politician whose family roots were in Foggia, he was a natural choice for the job.

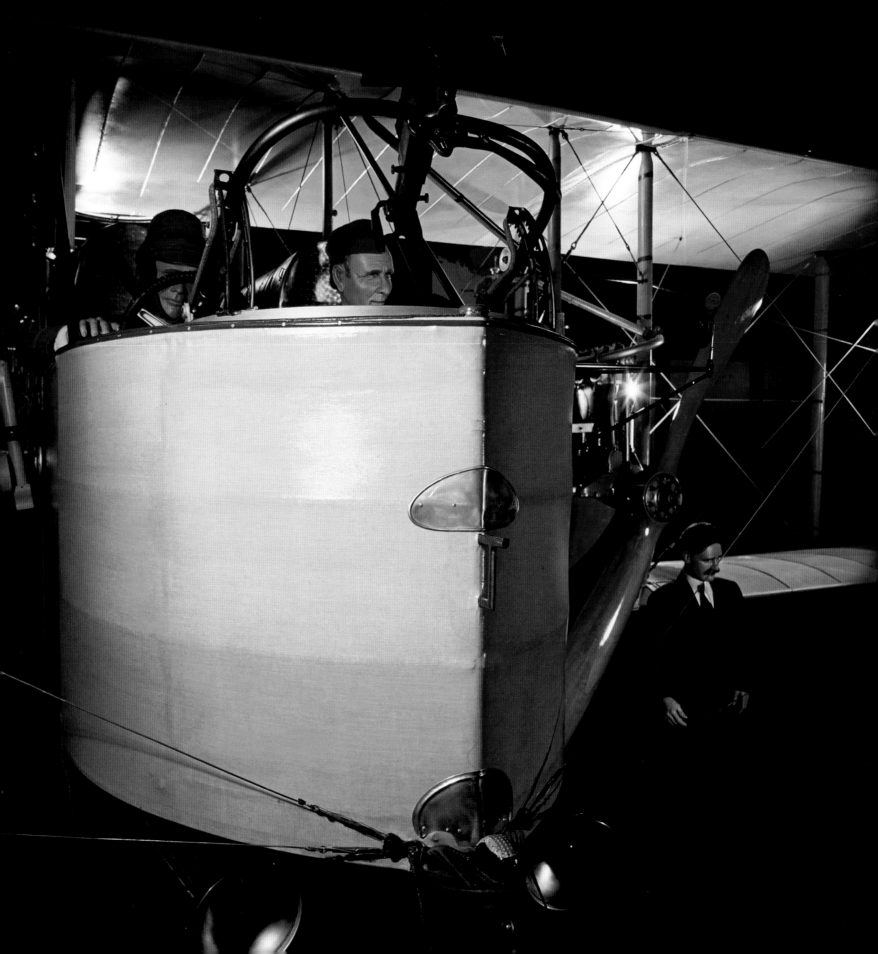

Right: The Ca. 36 at the National Museum of the USAF is on display to represent the first steps taken by American airmen in establishing a strategic air power doctrine. The giant biplane was powered by large Issotta-Fraschini engines and was flown by two pilots in an open cockpit. The bomber had no trim controls which relieve the pressure on the flying controls, meaning the pilots had to "hand fly" the big bomber for exhausting lengths of time. **Below:** The Caproni Ca.42 triplane was a huge twin-boomed machine of almost 100-foot wingspan. It could carry nearly two tons of bombs in the container beneath the crew nacelle. Cruising at 80 miles per hour, the Ca.42 could stay airborne for seven hours.

Over 400 Americans graduated from the Italian school by the end of the war. The big Caproni was an effective first step on the road to strategic bombing. It could carry almost 2,000 pounds of bombs and had a range of nearly 400 miles. Its American crews, however, acknowledged that it was slow and not very sophisticated. It was flat out at 85 miles per hour, and the absence of trimming controls made it an exhausting aircraft to fly. All the big Capronis were tail-heavy, and it was reported that "you had literally to jam your elbow into your stomach and hold the stick forward with one hand while you operated the ailerons with the other." The instruments were pretty basic, too. One pilot remembered that: "The air speed indicator was a rough and ready affair consisting of what we called a 'penny on a string,' a little round disc on a spring on one of the struts outside the cockpit. When the wind was blowing on it, it was blown backwards, and when the wind wasn't so strong, it came forwards. Behind it was a plate on which were the two words 'Minima' and 'Maxima.' If you let it get below 'Minima' you stalled, and if you got above 'Maxima' the wings fell off."

From June 1918, American pilots were assigned to Italian squadrons where they were integrated with Italian crews to fly bombing missions against Austrian targets. Almost one hundred Americans served in the battle area and took part in sixty-five raids, mostly at night. Relatively small and brief though the Italian program was, it was invaluable in providing the U.S. Air Service with its first combat experience in the strategic bombing role.

Left: In Caproni bombers, the rear gunner occupied a precarious and exposed railed platform mounted over the central engine and just clear of its whirling propellor. **Above:** Bill Marsalko's painting of Capronis over the Alps captures the essence of long-range Italian operations against the Austrians. Crews were exposed to below-zero air for hours in the open cockpits of these heavily loaded bombers.

Sopwith Camel

World War I's Most Successful Fighter

BY THE TIME THE SOPWITH CAMEL began arriving in frontline squadrons in May 1917, it was apparent that the little biplane was a formidable fighter aircraft. Six months later, Camels were being flown by nine RFC and six RNAS squadrons in France, two RFC squadrons in Italy, and another in the United Kingdom. More than 3,400 Camels had been ordered and production was underway in nine factories.

The Camel was not as much without vice as was its predecessor, the Pup. It was tricky to fly because of its small size and the considerable gyroscopic effect from its rotary engine during maneuvers. In a sharp turn to the left, the nose rose abruptly and had to be checked by coarse use of rudder, or the Camel would very quickly spin without warning. On the other hand, it was extremely maneuverable in the hands of a competent pilot, and it would turn to the right quicker than any other machine. Many of its pilots came to think of it as unquestionably the greatest plane on the front and there is some weight behind that opinion. Many of the war's greatest aces were Camel pilots, including Raymond Collishaw (62 victories), D.R. MacLaren (54), W.G. Barker (54) and H.W. Woollett (35). On one occasion, Woollett destroyed six aircraft in the course of a single day. Between the time of its introduction in 1917 and the end of the war, the Camel was the victor in more aerial combats than any other aircraft on either side — a total of 1,294 enemy aircraft destroyed — and so, in spite of its shortcomings, it has a claim to be considered the fighting scout supreme.

By the summer of 1918, the Camel was not quite the dominant fighter it once had been. With a top speed of 115 miles per hour, it

The Sopwith Camel shot down more aircraft (1,294) than any other fighter in World War I. **Opposite:** The Camel on display at the National Museum of the USAF is in the markings of Lieutenant George A. Vaughan of the 17th Aero Squadron. He was the fourth-ranking U.S. ace of WWI, with 13 victories.

was among the slowest of the fighters and this sometimes proved an embarrassment when it was used on escort duty, because the RFC's D.H.9 bombers were faster than Camels both when flying level and in the dive. One pilot claimed that "A Camel pilot had to shoot down every German plane in the sky in order to get home himself, as the Camel could neither outclimb nor outrun a Fokker."

A navalized version of the Camel was the 2F.1, the ultimate WWI shipboard fighter. It was similar to its land-based cousin but had a fuselage that could be broken in half behind the cockpit to facilitate stowage on board. Once the British fleet had the Camel, the concern about the presence of Zeppelins was much diminished. Camels struck some heavy blows at the German airships, two of them in ways unconventional for the little fighter. On July 19, 1918, seven Camels took off from HMS *Furious* near the coast of Schleswig-Holstein and attacked the Zeppelins in their lair at Tondern. Zeppelins L.54 and L.60 were destroyed by 50-pound bombs. Only three of the Camel pilots were recovered by the ship; three were interned in Denmark and one was drowned. Five of the seven Camels were lost, but that was judged a small price to pay for two Zeppelins.

The second operation was the result of a parallel development for taking aircraft to sea. On August 11, 1918, using a lighter originally intended for towing flying boats, a Camel flown by Sub-Lieutenant Stuart Culley was launched from behind a destroyer steaming at 30 knots. It was airborne after rolling just five feet. Culley climbed for nearly an hour to reach 18,000 feet, close to his ceiling, only to find that Zeppelin L.53 was still several hundred feet above him. At this point, the German captain altered course and passed

over the Camel on a reciprocal heading. Culley dragged the stick fully back and managed to empty a Lewis gun drum into the massive belly of the airship before his aircraft stalled and fell away. Flames erupted from the L.53, reducing it to its skeletal frame in seconds. It was the last airship to be shot down in WWI. In cloudy weather, it took an increasingly anxious Culley some time to sight his parent destroyer. Once it was found, however, he allowed himself an exuberant roll or two over the ship and ditched the

Camel alongside with only a pint of fuel remaining. The ditching was so smoothly done that the aircraft was recovered intact and is now part of the collection at the Imperial War Museum in London.

A signal to the Admiralty recording the L.53's destruction by Culley's Camel said "Your attention is called to Hymn No. 224, Verse 7." Reference to *Hymns Ancient and Modern* revealed the message as: "O Happy band of pilgrims, Look upward to the skies, Where such a light affliction, Shall win so great a prize."

Above: Sopwith Camel B6362 of 28 Squadron, RFC, being examined by French personnel in France, where Lieutenant J. H. Mitchell was credited with two victories over Albatros D.Vs on October 27, 1917. The pennants attached to the rear struts are those of a flight leader. B6362 was subsequently sent to Italy, where 2nd Lieutenant Harold Butler was credited with a shared victory over a kite balloon on December 28, 1917, and an Albatros D.III on February 20, 1918. Second Lieutenant A. G. Cooper was flying B6362 when he was credited with a shared Albatros D.III on December 29, 1917. B6362 failed to return from a patrol on February 22, 1918, and 2nd Lieutenant Butler was reported killed in action.

Left: The Sopwith Camel's cockpit was a simple affair with very few instruments. Twin Vickers machine guns were mounted above the engine, bracketing a basic sighting tube.

Opposite: Powered by a 130-horsepower Clerget rotary engine, the Camel was not among the fastest WWI fighters. Its maximum speed at sea level was only 117 miles per hour. However, it was one of the most maneuverable and became the war's highest-scoring fighter, shooting down 1,294 enemy aircraft. The twin guns were synchronized to fire through the whirling propeller.

Fokker D.VII

Too Few and Too Late

WHEN IT APPEARED IN MAY 1918, the Fokker D.VII soon showed its fighting qualities. With its excellent handling characteristics and higher ceiling than Allied fighters, German pilots found that they had a machine that could more than match their enemies and were able to score 565 victories during August 1918 alone. It was viceless, a steady gun platform, and had the best rate of climb of any combat aircraft on either side. With some justification, it was claimed that it could make good pilots out of mediocre material.

Designed by Reinhold Platz, the D.VII was selected in preference to several other designs during a competition held in January and February 1918. Manfred von Richthofen tested the prototype and initially reported that it was tricky, unpleasant, and directionally unstable in a dive. In response to his comments, Fokker lengthened the fuselage and added a fixed fin in front of the rudder. After flying the modified fighter, Richthofen praised it as the best aircraft in the competition. He found it easy to fly, rock steady at high speed and with good visibility from the cockpit. His approval effectively decided matters and Fokker were awarded a contract. To achieve high production rates, Fokker, the Albatross company, and the Allgemeine Elektrizitats Gesellschaft (A.E.G.) all manufactured D.VIIs. By the end of the war in November 1918, more than 1,700 aircraft had been built.

As the German offensives slowed in 1918 and they were driven irrevocably onto the defensive, the air battles remained intense. After starting the year with the Albatros D.V and the Fokker Dr.1 Triplane, which had difficulty in matching the Allied fighters, the Luftstreitkräfte was given new heart by the arrival of the Fokker D.VII. It was not as fast as the SPAD XIII or the S.E.5a, but it was very maneuverable and could count on having a superior rate of climb at all altitudes. It could also could dive at high speed without any fear of structural failure. Unlike the Camel and SPAD, which stalled sharply and spun vigorously, the D.VII was remarkably docile and reluctant to spin. Although the D.VII Jastas were able, under leaders such as Ernst Udet and Hermann Göring, to score heavily against their enemies, they were overwhelmed by increasingly superior numbers. Richthofen's Flying Circus, now under Göring's command, fought almost to destruction and was withdrawn from the front. Well mounted and well led though they were, German fighter pilots were swamped by the rising tide of Allied manpower and industrial strength.

Richthofen died only days before the D.VII was introduced and never flew it in combat. Other pilots quickly racked up victories and praised the design. The Fokker D.VII's thick wing section endowed the airplane with good stall characteristics. Positioning below and behind a two-seater, where the enemy observer could not bring his guns to bear, a D.VII pilot could safely put his airplane into a nose-high attitude, with full power, in a nearly stalled condition. The ability of the D.VII to perform this maneuver made it a highly feared opponent in combat. Among the aces who took full advantage of the D.VII's fighting capabilities during the closing weeks of the war were Ernst Udet (62 victories), Erich Löwenhardt (54), Rudolph Berthold (44), Bruno Loerzer (44), Franz Büchner (40), Paul Bäumer (43), Lothar von Richthofen (40) and Hermann Göring (22).

After the war, the victorious Allies required the Germans to

Ernst Udet's sixty-two victories made him second only to Richthofen on the German aces list. When he had only six victories, his guns jammed during a dogfight with the great French ace Georges Guynemer, who saluted and turned away.
Opposite: The D.VII exhibited at the Musée de l'Air, le Bourget, is in the standard German camouflage pattern.

When it appeared in the latter stages of the war, the Fokker D.VII did not look very different from other fighters, but it soon acquired a fearsome reputation. The Fokker D.VII on display at the National Museum of the USAF is finished in the exotic lavender color scheme adopted by Lieutenant Rudolph Stark of Jasta 35.

hand over all remaining examples of the D.VII. Although operational for only a short time, it had gained a fearsome reputation among Allied air forces and was the only machine specifically mentioned by name in the armistice agreement. However, about 120 examples of the type were smuggled into Holland, where Fokker set up shop and continued to produce aircraft. The U.S. Army brought 142 D.VIIs back to the United States and used them as Air Service trainers for many years. Twelve D.VIIs were transferred to the U.S. Navy, and the U.S. Marine Corps operated six of these aircraft until 1924. As a result the D.VII influenced the design of several later U.S. Navy fighters, including the Boeing FB-1, which entered service in 1925.

Above: Seen from the side, the simple design of the Fokker D.VII is readily apparent. A boxy fuselage ends in a dorsal strake and a small rudder. Reacting to Richthofen's criticism of the original prototype, the D.VII had the strake added and the fuselage lengthened to improve the handling qualities. **Right:** Manfred von Richthofen flew the Fokker D.VII during trials, but never in combat. He found it easy to fly and praised the excellent view from the cockpit, which, even by 1918, was still not overburdened with instruments. Hard to miss were the cocking levers for the two Spandau machine guns directly in front of the pilot.

SPAD XIII

French and Fast

THE SPAD XIII WAS DESIGNED IN 1916. The firepower of the earlier and very popular SPAD VII (the name SPAD is from Societe pour l'Aviation et ses Derives / Society for Aviation and its Derivatives) was doubled by using two Vickers 303 machine guns with 400 rounds each. The enthusiasm of the French pilots who tested the aircraft between April and September 1917 encouraged the French government to place an initial order for more than 2,000. The U.S. Air Service began flying the SPAD XIII in March 1918 and by the end of the war the U.S. had acquired 893. The SPAD XIII more than held its own against German aircraft until summer 1918, when it was challenged by the new Fokker D.VII. Rugged and fast for its day, the SPAD XIII was one of the most capable fighters of the war, and one of the most produced, with 8,472 built. Eighty-one French and Allied Squadrons were equipped with the type before the end of WWI.

The SPAD XIII was faster than its contemporaries and renowned for its ruggedness and diving ability, however its maneuverability was inferior, especially at low speeds. Poor gliding characteristics and a very sharp stall made it a difficult aircraft for novice pilots to handle. However, it could withstand the stress of dives at over 250 miles per hour and was at its best when used in slashing hit-and-run attacks rather than the tight turns of a dogfight. It was a very stable firing platform and was tough enough to absorb more than its share of punishment. An unusual feature was the main fuel tank, which was fitted at the bottom of the fuselage and had an emergency release system.

Edward Vernon Rickenbacker achieved six aerial victories in 1918 while flying Nieuports, then was grounded by illness, but returned to action flying the aircraft he most admired, the SPAD XIII. By war's end he was the leading American ace with 26 kills.
Opposite: At the Italian Air Force Museum, Vigna di Valle, is a SPAD VII flown by Ernesto Cabruna, an eight-victory ace, while he was with the 77th Squadriglia in 1918.

Many fighter aces either consolidated or made their reputations in combat while flying the SPAD XIII, including Charles Nungesser (45 victories) and René Fonck, the leading Allied ace (75). Fonck was never wounded and claimed that only one enemy bullet ever hit his aircraft. He was meticulous in his preparations for combat and an expert shot who took pride in using as few rounds as possible in shooting down an enemy. An excellent pilot, he was inclined to be boastful and self-promoting. He neither drank nor relaxed with other pilots, preferring to spend his time planning missions, pressing his uniforms, and keeping fit. His skill and his boastfulness were exemplified by his remark: "I put my bullets into the target as if by hand." Even those who were close to him found him hard to live with, and one pilot wrote that "[Fonck] is a tiresome braggart, and even a bore — but in the air, a slashing rapier, a steel blade tempered with unblemished courage and priceless skill…. But afterwards he can't forget how he rescued you, nor let you forget it. He can almost make you wish he hadn't helped you in the first place."

The S.XIII was also flown by the American fighter aces Eddie Rickenbacker and Frank Luke. Attacking balloons was dangerous, since they were heavily defended. The most successful balloon buster was Frank Luke. Between September 12 and 29, 1918, while flying with the 27th Squadron, Luke shot down 14 balloons and four aircraft. His meteoric and often undisciplined career ended on the evening of September 29 when he subjected the Germans on the front near Verdun to a lone assault worthy of a Wagnerian epic. As the sun was setting, he flew over the American 7th Balloon Company and

dropped a note which warned them to "Watch for burning balloons." The first German balloon fell in flames at 7.05 P.M., and was rapidly followed by another. Luke was momentarily diverted by some harassing Fokkers and disposed of two of them before claiming his third balloon. At some point he was hit by ground fire and seriously wounded, but he turned to strafe German troops before crash-landing. Once on the ground, he dragged himself from the cockpit and died nearby, pistol in hand. Frank Luke was posthumously awarded the Medal of Honor.

Eddie Rickenbacker achieved his early kills flying Nieuports, but he is particularly remembered for flying the SPAD XIII.

Heavier and not nearly so maneuverable as the Nieuport, nor its formidable adversary the Fokker D.VII, the SPAD was a fighter that suited Rickenbacker's style of aerial combat perfectly. He described it as "more impressive than any other airplane, any automobile, any other piece of equipment I had ever seen…the ultimate aircraft in the war in which aviation developed."

Rickenbacker had gained six victories before an ear infection grounded him for much of June, July and August 1918. He joined the 94th in mid-September and was made squadron commander a few days later. Older than most fighter pilots at 28, he was a mature and thoughtful leader, much respected by his men. In the air, he was nerveless and calculating, taking time to maneuver the

Above: A look inside the SPAD XIII at the National Museum of the USAF reveals that the simple cockpit instrumentation was neatly arranged on a narrow facia at shoulder level. Windscreens were rudimentary affairs, but in the SPAD the heavy framing could not have helped the pilot's field of vision. **Right:** The undercarriage and timeless Michelin tires of the Italian Museum's SPAD. **Opposite:** Suspended in the Musée de l'Air at Le Bourget is a famous aircraft — the SPAD VII *Vieux Charles* in which Georges Guynemer achieved 18 of his aerial victories. Less maneuverable than their contemporaries, SPADS were faster and quicker in climbing to height. Pilots used to tightly turning dogfights in other aircraft were slow to appreciate their qualities, but in time developed tactics that made its superiority clear.

tactical situation in his favor rather than rushing headlong into combat. Like most great aces, he believed in getting in close to his enemy, firing one solid burst, and then breaking away, ever watchful for the surprise attack from behind.

On his first day as squadron commander, Rickenbacker gave a demonstration of his skill. He set off on a hunting expedition and sighted two LVG observation aircraft escorted by five Fokkers. Placing himself above them and into sun, he dived onto the last Fokker and despatched it with one burst. As the escorts broke in confusion, Rickenbacker kept his dive going for

the LVGs. After exchanging fire with the rear gunners, he slipped out to one side of the pair and ruddered his SPAD so that the nearer LVG flew through his line of fire. Rickenbacker himself colorfully described the result: "It burst into flames and tumbled like a great blazing torch to earth, leaving a streamer of black smoke against the blue sky." He went on to score a total of 26 kills (22 aircraft and four balloons), becoming America's leading ace of WWI. In 1931, Rickenbacker's exploits were finally recognized formally and he belatedly became the fourth airman to be awarded the Medal of Honor.

Curtiss NC-4

First Across the Pond

LORD NORTHCLIFFE OF THE *Daily Mail,* a leading sponsor of aviation, ignited public excitement in 1913 by offering £10,000 for the first nonstop flight between the British Isles and North America. At the time, no aircraft was capable of covering the 1,800 miles separating Newfoundland and Ireland, nor could engines be counted on to keep running for twenty hours or more. Lord Northcliffe, however, believed in stimulating aeronautical advance by setting goals beyond current capabilities, and it was not long before his challenge was accepted. Two companies, Martin and Handasyde (later Martinsyde) in Britain and Curtiss in the United States, designed and built aircraft for the Atlantic crossing. The death of the Martinsyde's pilot and the onset of WWI prevented prewar attempts being made.

Lord Northcliffe had a reputation as a visionary, but it was a surprise when, in July 1918, with the issue on the western front still far from settled, he announced in the *Daily Mail* that the transatlantic prize would be renewed, excluding only airmen and aircraft of the soon-to-be defeated Central Powers. With the signing of the Armistice in November, aviators on both sides of the Atlantic were quick to turn their attentions to conquering the ocean barrier. Preparations were underway by the spring of 1919, with aircraft from Handley Page, Vickers, Boulton-Paul, Fairey, Shorts, Sopwith and Martinsyde among the British entries. In the United States, a floatplane designed by the Witteman-Lewis company was being readied, and the U.S. Navy decided to make an official transatlantic effort. The Navy, however, declined to be drawn into the mercenary world of the *Daily Mail's* competition, declaring that it would be ethically improper for the USN to enter the contest when backed by all the resources of a national exchequer. They elected instead to continue with a wartime project already in hand and to be content with "the immortal honor of being first."

The aircraft chosen by the U.S. Navy was a Curtiss flying boat, conceived for maritime patrol duties in European waters but produced too late to see wartime use. Four NC class flying boats were built (Navy Curtiss, generally known as "Nancies"). The end of the war removed the requirement for European operations, but the Navy remained interested in establishing an aerial transatlantic link. Preparations were entrusted to Commander John Towers, who planned a route from Newfoundland to England via the Azores and Portugal. The NC's cruising range of 1,470 miles ruled out a nonstop flight. Three aircraft were made available to attempt the crossing. Each carried a crew of six, and had both radio and radio direction-finding equipment on board. The plan included the deployment of 66 USN ships stationed at intervals along the intended track from Long Island to southwest England, available to give weather reports, provide navigational assistance, and carry out rescues.

Glenn Curtiss was the first to design and build successful large flying boats. In 1914, he built the twin-engined *America.* **Opposite:** The NC-4 inside the National Museum of Naval Aviation, Pensacola, produced too late for use in WWI, was one of four flying boats that gave the U.S. Navy the chance to attempt an Atlantic crossing in May 1919. Only NC-4 survived.

On May 8, 1919, NC-1, NC-3 and NC-4 left Long Island for Trepassey Bay, Newfoundland, commanded respectively by Lieutenant Commander Patrick Bellinger, Commander Towers, and Lieutenant Commander Albert Read. NC-4 was forced down on the sea by engine trouble on the way, and Read's crew spent several uncomfortable hours taxiing for 80 miles to reach Chatham, near Cape Cod. Read rejoined the formation at Trepassey Bay on May 15 and the three flying boats lifted off on

Above: The Navy Curtiss NC-4 flying boat was a typical Curtiss three-bay, strut-and-wire-braced biplane with a short, wide-beam, single-step hull. The tail assembly was supported by wire-braced outriggers extending back from the top wing and the stern of the hull. This arrangement was chosen to minimize hull weight and place the tail high above the waves in rough seas. Power was supplied by four 400-horsepower Liberty engines, mounted in three nacelles. Two of the engines were in a tractor-pusher arrangement in the center. The wooden frame of the short, broadbeam hull was covered on the sides and bottom with two layers of planking that were glued together with a sheet of canvas in between and had a three-ply wood veneer turtle deck. **Left:** In 1919, one of the "Nancies" (NC-1) held the record for number of passengers carried — 51 (including one stowaway). Servicing the big flying boat was a major operation, as can be judged from the number of navy men working on the NC-4 in this photograph.

the first leg of their epic flight, 1,300 miles to the Azores, on the following evening. Bad weather soon enveloped them. They flew on separately, but heavy clouds and low ceilings denied them a sight both of the sea and of star-shells fired by ships as tracking aids. With the weather worsening, both NC-1 and NC-3 were forced to exchange one unfriendly element for another, each splashing down into rough seas and suffering damage. After five hours of drifting, the men from NC-1 were rescued by the Greek freighter *Ionia*, but their aircraft was abandoned to a watery grave. Commander Towers in NC-3 was determined to reach the Azores. Drifting and taxiing for some 200 miles in the next 53 hours, he struggled into Ponta Delgada on the island of Sao Miguel, steadfastly refusing the offer of a tow from the destroyer *Harding* over the last few miles. Missing both wing pontoons, most of the lower wing fabric and part of the tail, the battered NC-3 would go no further.

Meanwhile, NC-4 battled through the storms and survived the worst the weather could do. On the morning of May 17, a relieved crew sighted the island of Flores. The weather was still appalling, so Read, well short of the intended destination of Ponta Delgada, put his aircraft down at Horta on Fayal. The NC-4 had covered 1,380 miles in 15 hours and 13 minutes, an average speed of 90 miles per hour. Compared with the drama of the first leg, the rest of the crossing was anticlimactic. Read moved on to Ponta Delgada and, after resting his men and their machine, took NC-4 to Lisbon, touching down on the Tagus River on May 27, 1919, after a flight of nine hours and 44 minutes. The Atlantic had been crossed by air for the first time.

Four days later, Read's crew and their flying boat arrived in Plymouth harbor, near where the Pilgrim Fathers set sail from England in 1620. They had covered 4,320 miles since leaving Long Island and had spent 53 hours and 58 minutes in the air. It was a memorable achievement, a tribute to the commitment of the U.S. Navy and to the determination of a thoroughly professional crew of naval airmen.

Above: The NC-4 arriving at her anchorage at Ponta Delgada, Azores, May 20, 1919. The NC-4 was a large aircraft, with a gross weight of 27,386 pounds and a wingspan of 126 feet. The wing area of 2,380 square feet was only some 18 percent less than that of a Boeing 707.

Vickers Vimy

Nonstop Transatlantic

THE ATLANTIC HAD BEEN conquered in stages, but the £10,000 *Daily Mail* prize for the first nonstop crossing still had to be won. Among the hopefuls gathering in Newfoundland in 1919 were John Alcock and Arthur Whitten-Brown with their modified Vickers Vimy bomber. Extra fuel tanks had been fitted, bringing the capacity up to 865 imperial gallons, enough for 2,440 miles.

Facilities in Newfoundland were primitive, and the Vimy had to be prepared in the open, inadequately protected from the often unfriendly weather by canvas screens. While the aircraft was being assembled, Alcock searched for a takeoff field. Eventually, a meadow barely 400 yards long was cleared of rocks and trees. By June 8 the field was clear, but the weather was not. Gales and rain frustrated the waiting airmen until June 13, and then, when it seemed that they might get off at last, a shock absorber broke as the Vimy was being fueled. Mechanics worked all night on the problem and, on June 14, 1919, everything was ready.

Alcock and Brown were at the field before dawn, getting weather forecasts, loading navigation instruments and provisions, and accepting bags of special mail. The fuel had been strained through chamois leather, and the radiator water boiled and filtered. Alcock and Brown carried their lucky mascots, two stuffed toy cats, Lucky Jim and Twinkletoes. After eating lunch under the Vimy's wing, they climbed into the cockpit and started the engines. The Vimy was positioned as near the end of the field as possible, and Alcock had arranged for men to stand in front of the wing, holding the aircraft back as he opened up to full power. One of these improvised brakes later recalled that, at Alcock's signal,

Modified Vimy bombers featured in record-breaking flights. In February 1920, Lieutenant Colonel Pierre van Ryneveld (left) and Major C.J. Quintin-Brand took off from near London in a Vimy named *Silver Queen* in an attempt to become the first to fly from London to Cape Town. **Opposite:** In the London Science Museum's History of Flight gallery is the Vimy flown by John Alcock and Arthur Whitten-Brown in their 1919 first nonstop crossing of the Atlantic by air.

"we all sat down on the ground and the plane shot forward." The Vimy lumbered into the air at 16:13 GMT. For a few moments, the anxious onlookers held their breaths as Alcock kept the nose down to gain airspeed and the aircraft sank out of sight into a valley. All was well, however, and the Vimy crossed the coast of Newfoundland at 1,200 feet.

As they settled on a heading for Ireland, the wind-driven generator supplying power to the radio failed. Soon after that, Brown's electrically heated jacket failed, too, and the starboard engine's exhaust manifold broke away, the resulting roar making cockpit conversation impossible. Once the coast was left behind, Brown took his first sextant shots and measured the Vimy's drift, but it was not long before they were sandwiched between banks of cloud and further observations became impossible. They had been flying for eight hours before Alcock broke through the clouds and gave Brown a chance to fix their position. He calculated that they were close to their intended track and had covered 850 miles at a ground speed of 106 miles per hour.

The first light of dawn revealed solid walls of cloud across their path. The Vimy was thrown about by severe turbulence and ice formed on the wings, blocked the pitot tube and rendering the airspeed indicator and altimeter useless. Deprived of basic flying instruments, Alcock became disorientated. As he remembered it: "We lost our instinct of balance. The machine, left to its own devices, swung, flew amok, and began to perform circus tricks." In fact, the Vimy probably stalled before entering a spiral dive, losing height rapidly and breaking clear of the low cloud-base

Above: John Alcock (left) and Arthur Whitten-Brown in uniform after their epic transatlantic flight. Alcock did not enjoy his celebrity for long; he was killed in a Viking amphibian on December 18, 1919, attempting a forced landing in fog near Rouen, France. The car in this picture is a 10-horsepower Humber, and the man in the middle is Leonard Davies of the Humber Car Company. **Opposite:** Aerodynamically, the Vimy was a blunt instrument. The two 350-horsepower Rolls-Royce Eagle engines had to work hard to pull the forest of wires and struts along at a cruising speed of 90 miles per hour. Alcock and Brown endured the discomfort of an open cockpit during many hours of flying through stormy Atlantic weather.

frighteningly close to the sea in a steeply banked descending turn. Alcock recovered to level flight just in time and brought the aircraft back onto an easterly heading. Brown's impression was that he could almost have reached out and touched the wave tops.

Climbing again to find clear air, Alcock often had to move the controls briskly to break loose the ice which threatened to jam the ailerons. The fuel-flow gauges outside the cockpit iced over and several times Brown had to stand up in the biting gale to scratch them clear. Struggling up to 11,000 feet, they at last saw the sun, and Brown estimated that they were only 80 miles from land. Ice then built up in the engine intakes, and the starboard engine lost power. They had to descend into warmer air, going down to 500 feet before the engine regained its ear-shattering roar. Less than half an hour later they sighted small islands off the coast of Galway, and soon after saw the masts of Clifden radio station. Still faced by appalling weather and exhausted by over 16 hours in the air, Alcock decided to land, although there was enough fuel left to take them to London. He selected what appeared to be a grassy field and set-

tled the Vimy onto its surface, only to find that he had chosen an Irish bog. The wheels sank into the morass and the aircraft buried its nose deep in the soft mud. With its tail in the air and its nose pressed to the earth, the Vimy seemed to kissing the ground in gratitude for its safe arrival on the eastern side of the great ocean. Its Rolls-Royce Eagles had kept them in the air for 16 hours and 28 minutes (15 hours, 57 minutes coast to coast), hauling the angular airframe along for 1,890 miles at an average of 118 miles per hour.

Alcock and Brown had carved their names into aviation history as the first to fly the Atlantic nonstop. Crowds cheered them everywhere on their way to London, and their drive to a Royal Aero Club lunch in their honor became a triumphal procession. Winston Churchill, then Secretary of State for War and Air, was there to present them with their cheque from the *Daily Mail*, and the next day they were knighted by King George V. Wrapped in the nation's adulation, the airmen did not forget those who made their flight possible: £2,000 of the prize money was set aside to be shared out among the ground crew.

Douglas World Cruiser

Global Conquest

ONCE THE ATLANTIC HAD been conquered by the U.S. Navy's NC-4 and the Vickers Vimy of Alcock and Brown, airmen the world over thought about the possibility of flying round the world. The competition to be the first was international. In the United States, both the Navy and the Army had thought about the idea, but it was the Army's proposal that prevailed, primarily on the grounds of finding out more about operating over long distances and in different climates. Unspoken was the obvious point that success in such a venture would be good publicity for the Air Service.

Tasked with achieving global flight, the Army Air Service faced the challenge with professional thoroughness. Preparation included shipping spare parts and tools to various points along the route, getting clearances from the foreign governments involved, positioning rescue ships, and despatching officers to collect local information and arrange for supplies. It was also essential to obtain aircraft capable of getting the job done. The machines selected were designed by Donald Douglas, based on his rugged Liberty-engined DT-2 Navy floatplane. Five were ordered, four to make the flight plus one spare. The Douglas World Cruiser (DWC) was a big, two-seat, open-cockpit biplane with a fuel capacity of 450 gallons, enough for over 1,000 miles in still air. Since the DWC's cruising speed was not much more than 80 miles per hour, it was clear that the Army was prepared to take its time over the venture.

Led by Major Frederick Martin, the formation of four DWCs (*Seattle, Chicago, Boston* and *New Orleans*) left Seattle on April 6, 1924, and headed for Alaska. There they suffered a grievous blow

Douglas World Cruiser *Chicago* was flown by the leader of the U.S. Army's round-the-world flight, Lieutenant Lowell Smith. Here he is welcomed home after successfully crossing two oceans and two continents. **Opposite:** At the National Air and Space Museum, *Chicago* is a tribute to the sturdy Douglas design. In six months of flying, four World Cruisers were airborne for more than 360 hours in covering over 27,000 miles.

when *Seattle* crashed into a fog-obscured mountain on the long Alaskan Peninsula. Martin and his mechanic survived, and the flight continued west with three aircraft, now led by Lieutenant Lowell Smith, an aerial refueling pioneer. The first linking of the Americas to the Orient by air is often overlooked because it happened in the course of achieving the far larger goal of a round-the-world flight.

The Douglas World Cruisers took a route across the northern Pacific that hugged the coast of Alaska before hopping along the Aleutian island chain to Japan. It was not a simple affair. As Lieutenant Lowell Smith said: "We knew the trans-Pacific leg would be the worst of our flight, but it was ten times worse than we expected. Fog, snow, hail, wind, and more fog conspired to prevent us crossing the Pacific." From Seattle to the Japanese home islands took more than five weeks and involved massive support from vessels of the U.S. Navy and Coast Guard. Besides providing wonderful publicity for Army aviation, it was a stated aim of the flight "to point the way for all nations to develop aviation commercially." To some extent, this may have been accomplished, but the experimental nature of the enterprise was apparent from the need for the Army airmen to take their time over the short stages of the unfriendly northern route, and from the size of the supporting cast. It would be many years before aircraft acquired sufficient range, reliability and comfort to convince passengers that air travel was the preferred means of being transported between continents.

After reaching Japan, the route took the U.S. Army's pilots to China, India, Iraq and Turkey, and across Europe to the United Kingdom. After refitting for the Atlantic crossing, Lieutenant

Leigh Wade's *Boston* was lost through engine failure on the way to Iceland. Rescued by the USS *Richmond*, Wade and his mechanic were able to rejoin the flight in Newfoundland, where the spare DWC, now named *Boston II*, was waiting. However, that meant that only the crews of *Chicago* and *New Orleans* completed the first east-to-west heavier-than-air staged crossing of the Atlantic. Lieutenants Lowell Smith and Erik Nelson succeeded in closing the global circle on September 28, 1924, arriving back at Seattle 175 days and over 360 flying hours after they began. The 27,553 miles had been covered at an average speed of 74 miles per hour. Meticulous preparation combined with the professionalism and determination of the crews had brought the U.S. Army Air Service the honor of recording the first round-the-world flight.

Above: The Douglas World Cruisers replaced their wheels with pontoons for the long legs flown over water during their circumnavigation. Here Chicago rumbles past an older form of maritime transport. **Opposite:** Artifacts from the U.S. Army Air Service's 1924 flight round-the-world are preserved at the National Museum of the USAF, Dayton, Ohio. Among them are Leigh Wade's jacket, helmet and gloves, and John Harding's bible, diary and cigarette case. Erik Nelson is represented by a pennant given to him by a rival global airman, Antonio Locatelli of Italy.

Fokker World Beaters

Trimotors and Trailblazers

HAVING SUCCEEDED IN FLYING round the world in 1924, U.S. Army airmen also led the way to Hawaii in a landplane. On June 28, 1927, Lietenants Maitland and Hegenberger flew the Fokker C-2 *Bird of Paradise* the 2,400 miles from San Francisco to Oahu in 25 hours, 50 minutes. The advances in capability since 1924 were marked. Radio beacons were installed at the points of departure and arrival, and the C-2 had improved radios, an earth indicator compass, four magnetic compasses, and a drift sight. The meticulous preparations meant little to the sensation-seeking press, and newspaper reports dramatized the risks of the flight and the daring of the pilots. Hegenberger went out of his way to contradict the headlines: "Contrary to popular opinion, the significance of the Hawaiian flight was not the personal hazard involved but the triumph of careful preparation of the plane and equipment...." He drew attention to the Army's emphasis on flight safety and pointed out that the *Bird of Paradise* had fuel reserves sufficient for another 800 miles when it landed at Wheeler Field, Oahu.

While the *Bird of Paradise* was flying to Hawaii, the Australian airman Charles Kingsford-Smith was in California seeking sponsors for a transpacific flight. He had the money to buy the Fokker F.VIIb *Detroiter* used during a 1926 Arctic expedition. He was at the point of selling the aircraft to meet mounting debts when he met Allan Hancock, a millionaire shipbuilder. Hancock offered to buy the aircraft, now named *Southern Cross*, and lend it back for the transpacific attempt. With the enterprise thus secured, Kingsford-Smith showed his qualities as a professional airman. The *Southern Cross* was modified at the Douglas factory in Santa

The only flying example of a Fokker Super Universal. Rebuilt by Clark Seaborn of Calgary, Canada, it completed its first post-restoration flight on July 24, 1998. **Opposite:** Supported by the Western Canada Aviation Museum in Winnepeg, Manitoba, this yellow Fokker flew across the U.S. in the 2003 National Air Tour. Built with parts from four relics, this rare bird took 18 years and 10,000 hours' work for Seaborn and engineer Don McLean to rebuild.

Monica, and properly equipped to tackle the great ocean. The two standard compasses were joined by a master aperiodic compass and an earth inductor compass. There were sextants, two drift meters, and a blind flying panel fitted with the best instruments available. Kingsford-Smith spent hours in the air with the altimeter and airspeed indicators covered, practicing basic instrument flying. The navigator, Harry Lyon, trained himself in the use of a bubble sextant by taking shots while standing up in the back seat of a speeding open car on the coast road near San Francisco. The copilot, Charles Ulm, later described the measures taken to cope with the ultimate emergency: "We fitted a dump valve which would drop the bulk of our gasoline load in 50 seconds. We carried steel saws that would enable us to cut off the outboard motor and steel fuselage and turn the wing into a raft. In the wing we placed emergency rations, a still to condense water, and a watertight radio transmitter. Four gas balloons were carried to lift the aerial of this transmitter."

On May 31, 1928, they took off from Oakland airport. Twenty-seven hours later the *Southern Cross* was welcomed to the Hawaiian Islands by an aircraft escort that included the *Bird of Paradise*, flown by Lowell Smith of the U.S. Army's round-the-world flight. An incident shortly before they reached Hawaii offered some insight into one of the perils facing oceanic fliers. A small island was reported to the left of the aircraft's track. It should not have been there and it suggested that Lyon's navigation was off the mark. They altered course, only to find that the "island" was a cloud and its shadow. How many other aviators, searching desperately for a landfall, had

Charles Kingsford-Smith's *Southern Cross,* the aircraft that completed the first crossing of the Pacific by air in 1928. The Fokker F.VIIb-3m was extensively modified with the best instruments available and carried comprehensive survival gear. It is now on display at the Brisbane, Australia, airport.

been, and later would be, led by cloud illusions into chasing shadows until the fuel ran out?

The second leg of the flight was to Suva in the Fiji Islands, 3,200 miles away. To give Kingsford-Smith the longest possible takeoff run with a full fuel load of 1,300 gallons, the *Southern Cross* was ferried across to the 4,500-foot runway of Kauai's Barking Sands. He got the aircraft airborne with 1,000 feet to spare but then took six minutes to struggle up to 300 feet. Storms made things uncomfortable for several hours, particularly for the pilots, drenched by torrential rain in their open cockpit. Battered by turbulence and slowed by strong winds, after more than 30 hours in the air, they were exhausted. Tired as he was, Kingsford-Smith had to land the big trimotor in Fiji on a hastily prepared 1,300-foot strip on a sports ground. Without brakes, he did well to bring the aircraft to a stop with a deliberate ground loop at the end of the landing roll. The *Southern Cross* had been in the air for thirty-four and a half hours and there were just 30 gallons left in the fuel tanks.

The final leg of the flight was supposed to be the easiest. Fiji to Brisbane is only 1,900 miles and Lyon felt that even an amateur navigator could find Australia. It proved more of a challenge than they thought. Taking off from another beach, Kingsford-Smith was soon battling the worst weather he had ever experienced: "The visibility dwindled to a mile, then to a few yards, then to nothing. Torrential rain began to drum and rattle on the windshield.... Raking gusts jolted the plane so that we had to hold on to our seats." The awful conditions persisted for most of the flight, and by the time they abated, Lyon had no idea of their position. Testing his belief that Australia was too big to miss, he suggested steering due west. They crossed the Australian coast more than 100 miles off course. Their welcome when they landed at Brisbane's Eagle Farm airport was suitably ecstatic. The first crossing of the Pacific by air had occupied more than eight days and taken 83 hours and 15 minutes flying time.

Being the first to fly across the Pacific was reward enough, but the icing on the cake came in a congratulatory message from their American benefactor, Allan Hancock. His cable included news of a remarkable gesture: "I am delivering to the California Bank of Los Angeles for transmission to the Commercial Banking Company of Sydney a bill of sale transferring to Kingsford-Smith and Ulm the *Southern Cross* together with release and discharge of all your indebtedness to me." For the moment, the two Australian airmen were on top of the world.

The *Bird of Paradise* arriving in Hawaii after crossing the Pacific, a flight of 2,416 miles in 26 hours, 49 minutes. The Fokker C-2 was flown from California by U.S. Army Air Corps pilots Maitland and Hegenberger in June 1927.

Ryan NYP

Ninety-Second but Still First

IN 1919, RAYMOND ORTEIG, a French-born hotel owner in New York, announced that he would award a prize of $25,000 "to the first aviator of any Allied country crossing the Atlantic in one flight, from Paris to New York or New York to Paris." By 1926, aircraft had improved sufficiently to generate interest in the challenge and in September of that year the famous French ace, René Fonck, and his crew (Curtin, Clavier and Islamov) arrived at Roosevelt Field, New York, to attempt the crossing in a Sikorsky S.35. Fueled with the 2,380 gallons needed to cross the Atlantic, it was 10,000 pounds above its designed weight. Fonck, keen to be off, elected not to fly overweight tests scheduled by Sikorsky. On September 20, the takeoff run began on Roosevelt Field's mile long runway. The S.35 never looked as if it would get airborne. It struck a gully at the edge of the airfield and burst into flame. Fonck and Curtin scrambled clear, but Clavier and Islamov were burned to death. They were the first to pay the ultimate penalty for challenging the Atlantic by air, but they would not be the last.

With Fonck eliminated, there were five principal contenders. This was reduced to three during two disastrous weeks in the spring of 1927. On April 26, Noel Davis and Stanton Wooster were killed when their overweight Keystone Pathfinder crashed on takeoff from Langley Field, Virginia. Two weeks later, the French crew of Charles Nungesser and Francois Coli left Paris to attempt the first nonstop east-to-west crossing of the North Atlantic in their Levasseur PL-8 *L'Oiseau Blanc*. No reliable trace of the aircraft or its crew was ever found.

Charles Lindbergh stands in front of the *Spirit of St. Louis* holding a "Keep Out" sign modified to add "of the water."
Opposite: The engine of choice for trail-blazing aviators of the 1920s was the nine-cylinder Wright Whirlwind radial.
In the *Spirit of St. Louis,* the Whirlwind and its fuel tank filled the nose, leaving no room for a windscreen. Lindbergh could see forward only through a persicope.

Most observers now believed that the race for the Orteig prize lay between two of the three remaining aircraft and crew combinations. Either had the capacity to succeed, and one of them gave ample proof of that over Long Island in April. Clarence Chamberlin and Bert Acosta kept the Bellanca W.B.2 *Columbia* flying for more than fifty-one hours, which was more than enough to capture the Orteig prize. The other team was led by Commander Richard Byrd, USN, in the Fokker F.VIIb-3m *America.* Byrd and his sponsors insisted that they were not influenced by the prize, but their active preparations made them competitors in the eyes of everyone else.

The third remaining contestant was the comparatively unknown Charles Lindbergh, who proposed to take on the daunting challenge solo. Having been a barnstormer and air mail pilot, he was no beginner, but his Ryan NYP *Spirit of St. Louis* (an M-2 mail plane, modified to his specifications in just sixty days) was an unknown quantity. Lindbergh had kept a close eye on its construction, saving weight by eliminating any item he considered unessential. He had no radio and the instrument panel was without such luxuries as fuel gauges. The fuel used by the Wright Whirlwind radial was calculated from knowing the engine rpm and keeping track of time in the air. Lindbergh even kept his rations to a minimum, taking just five sandwiches and a canteen of water to sustain him for a flight lasting a day and a half. The weight saved was converted into fuel, 2,500 pounds of which was carried by an aircraft totaling little more than 5,000 pounds fully loaded. Most was in a tank that filled the fuselage from top to bottom between the engine and the cockpit, denying the pilot any forward view.

On May 12, 1927, the *Spirit of St. Louis* landed at Curtiss Field, Long Island. Worries about the limitations of Curtiss Field were overcome when Richard Byrd offered the use of the long runway at Roosevelt Field. A week later, a high pressure system over the Atlantic promised clear skies for most of the route. Lindbergh tried to rest for a few hours, but was with his aircraft before sunrise to see it towed through drizzling rain to Roosevelt Field. At 7:40 A.M. he started the engine and at 7:52 A.M. on May 20, 1927, the *Spirit of St. Louis* began to move. Agonizingly slowly, it gathered speed. The tail was up at the halfway point and the aircraft hopped once or twice before lifting to clear wires at the edge of the airfield. Lindbergh coaxed the *Spirit of St. Louis* up to cruising speed and settled down to the monotony of flying in long straight lines while sitting still behind the unchanging roar of a radial engine. By mid-Atlantic, he had hardly slept for two days, and the need to close his eyes was almost irresistible. Overcome by fatigue, he stopped keeping his log and became confused over when to make the scheduled heading changes needed to keep him on his great circle track.

After more than 24 hours, Lindbergh saw fishing boats before making landfall at Dingle Bay, Ireland, only three miles off his intended track. At dusk he reached Cherbourg and, as darkness fell, he picked up the gleam of airway beacons and followed them to Paris. Le Bourget airfield was not immediately obvious. Lindbergh finally decided that it must be a large dark area ringed by car headlights. Exhausted and with no forward vision, he still managed to put his aircraft down safely on an unfamiliar airfield in the dark.

Lindbergh was astonished by the exuberance of his welcome. He was pulled from his cockpit and passed from hand to hand over the heads of a mob. When an American newspaper correspondent was mistaken for him, Lindbergh was smuggled to the safety of the American Embassy where he borrowed a pair of pyjamas from the ambassador and fell asleep for the first time in more than two and a half days. He had achieved what few had thought possible, a solo flight from New York to Paris — 3,610 miles in thirty-three and a half hours. Ninety-one people had crossed the Atlantic by air before him, but he was the first to do it alone.

Above: The *Spirit of St. Louis* had no fuel gauge, so Lindbergh intended to calculate fuel consumption by knowing the rate per hour at which the Whirlwind used fuel at cruising speed and keeping a record of hours flown. The pencil marks he made on the plywood instrument panel as the hours passed are still there. **Left:** On the rudder of the *Spirit of St. Louis* the aircraft is identified as the Ryan NYP, letters chosen as an acronym for New York to Paris.

Lindbergh was determined not to carry an ounce of weight that was not essential, so the *Spirit of St. Louis* was stripped of everything that might be considered cosmetic. There were no panels to line the cockpit, no radio and no parachute. As the hours passed, he turned the valves in the tubing below the instrument panel to select fuel tanks in sequence. The periscope was viewed through the hole at the upper left of the panel, with the lever controlling the periscope's limited movement to its left.

Schneider Trophy Racers

Faster with Floats

IN 1913, JACQUES SCHNEIDER, a rich Frenchman who saw marine aircraft as the best hope for spanning oceans by air, established an international competition called the "Coupe d'Aviation Maritime Jacques Schneider" — the Schneider Trophy. It was intended to promote the development of practical aircraft, fast but with reasonable range, and capable of operating from the open sea with a useful payload. Until 1923, the competing aircraft (mostly flying boats) could be said to have been designed with Schneider's principles in mind, but in that year the contest was transformed to become an outright pursuit of speed.

The change in the Schneider Trophy's character in 1923 was brought about by the entry of a team from the U.S. Navy. The Navy airmen were experienced, disciplined pilots and they were backed by a thoroughly prepared support organization. Their Curtiss CR-3s were the technological wonders of the time, carrying the promise of awesome performance. From the moment they began their takeoff runs, it was clear that the race was theirs if they stayed in the air. The winner was Lieutenant David Rittenhouse, USN, at an average speed of 177.3 miles per hour. For those Europeans who had thought that claims made for American aircraft were exaggerated, the results were a rude shock. It was clear that the world's fastest aircraft were now being made on the western side of the Atlantic.

The U.S. success was repeated over Chesapeake Bay in 1925, when Lieutenant Jimmy Doolittle of the U.S. Army Air Service gave a masterly display in his Curtiss R3C-2, winning at 232.6 miles per hour. With U.S. superiority confirmed, American aviators looked forward to claiming the Schneider Trophy for a third time in 1926, so gaining the trophy in perpetuity. Alas for their hopes, the

On display in London's Science Museum is La Coupe d'Aviation Maritime Jacques Schneider, also known as the Schneider Trophy or, less formally, the Flying Flirt.
Opposite: In the Flight gallery of London's Science Museum is Supermarine S6B S1595, the racing floatplane designed by R.J. Mitchell that secured the Schneider Trophy for Britain in 1931.

U.S. government declined to continue its support for racing aircraft. In Italy, Mussolini saw an opportunity to show the world that nothing was too difficult for a Fascist state. He instructed the Italian aircraft industry and the Regia Aeronautica to "win the Schneider Trophy at all costs." Against the odds, the Italians achieved a minor miracle, producing the Macchi M.39, a firmly braced scarlet monoplane with very clean lines. It proved to be very fast and was flown to victory at 246.5 miles per hour by Major Mario de Bernadi, so ensuring that the Schneider Trophy series would continue.

The last three races of the competition were held in 1927, 1929 and 1931, and they were dominated by teams from Italy's Regia Aeronautica and Britain's Royal Air Force. The Italians produced several startlingly imaginative machines, of which the most outrageous by far was the Piaggio-Pegna P.c.7, a high-wing monoplane fitted with hydrofoils. At rest, it floated with the wings on the surface of the water. The engine was intended to drive both a boat propeller aft and an airscrew in the nose. Clutches engaged one or the other depending upon the medium being traversed. The P.c.7 did get as far as behaving like a boat, but it was never driven fast enough to allow its wings to spread. That left Macchi as the principal Italian standard bearer.

The British challengers were designed by R.J. Mitchell of Supermarine Aviation. When the teams faced each other at Venice in 1927, Mitchell's Supermarine S.5s justified their promise, while the Macchi M.52s were neither as fast nor as reliable as their rivals, all three of them retiring with mechanical troubles. The RAF's Flight Lieutenant S.N. Webster came home the winner

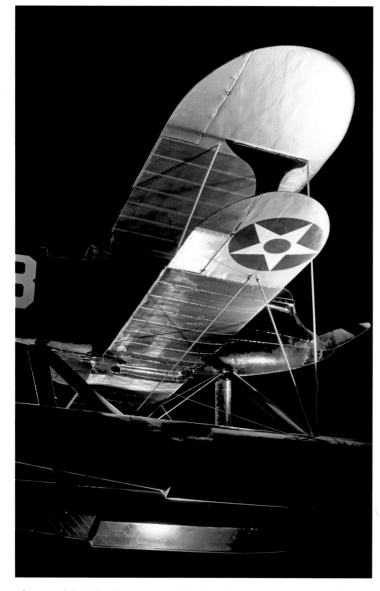

Above: Exhibited in the Pioneers of Flight gallery at the National Air & Space Museum, Washington, DC, is the Curtiss R3C-2 flown to victory in the 1925 Schneider Trophy race by Jimmy Doolittle. On the following day, Doolittle flew it again to set a new world record speed of 245.7 miles per hour. **Opposite:** The Macchi MC-72 is one of the most beautiful aircraft ever built, exuding elegance and power even when standing still. The ultimate achievement in racing floatplanes, it graces the collection of the Italian Air Force Museum at Vigna di Valle, on Lake Bracciano north of Rome. In 1934, flown by Francesco Agello and hurled along by a 3000-horsepower Fiat A.S.6 driving contra-rotating propellers, the MC-72 set a world air speed record of 440 miles per hour. To keep the massive A.S.6 from overheating, the surface of the MC-72 was covered in radiators — on the wings, struts and floats.

at 281.6 miles per hour. Cumbersome floats notwithstanding, intense competition had made racing floatplanes the fastest aircraft in the world.

In 1929, both Macchi and Supermarine fitted new engines. Macchi's M.67 used an 18-cylinder Isotta-Fraschini of 1800 horsepower, but it was not a happy marriage. The Supermarine S.6 had the new Rolls-Royce R engine, which produced 1850 horsepower. During the race, both M.67s were forced to retire, one because the pilot was choking on oily exhaust smoke, and the other when a radiator pipe burst, spraying scalding water into the cockpit. The winner at 328.63 miles per hour was the RAF's Flying Officer H.R.D. Waghorn.

With permanent possession of the Schneider Trophy within reach, the British government followed the example of the United States and announced that further involvement of Britain in the Schneider Trophy would have to be left to private enterprise. When all seemed lost, a fairy godmother appeared. Dame Lucy Houston, the eccentric widow of a shipping millionaire, offered £100,000 "To prevent the British government being spoilsports...." Mitchell modified his successful S.6 and asked Rolls-Royce to squeeze more power out of the "R" engine. The output was duly boosted to an impressive 2300 horsepower. Macchi more than matched this with the Fiat A.S.6, which was two A.S.5 engines bolted back to back to form a power unit 11 feet long. This supercharged monster, the A.S.6, produced 3000 horsepower, and it was housed in the MC.72, the ultimate in racing floatplanes. To handle the enormous power, the A.S.5 elements drove separate coaxial propeller shafts turning contra-rotating propellers. The combination ran beautifully on the ground, but in the air the MC.72 blew up and killed two of its pilots. In the circumstances, Italy submitted a formal request for a postponement. For Britain, however, with Lady Houston's money spent, it was now or never, so the request was denied.

On September 13, 1931, Flight Lieutenant John Boothman flew his S.6B (S1595) over the required seven laps, the "R" engine never faltering. He recorded an average speed of 340 miles per hour and gave Britain the Schneider Trophy in perpetuity. The British had made the most of the Schneider Trophy experience. Mitchell's work on the aerodynamics of the low-wing monoplane led to his superb Spitfire. The "R" engine fathered the famous Merlin, which powered not only the Spitfire, but also the Hurricane, Lancaster, Mosquito and the P-51 Mustang, all of which made powerful contributions to Allied air power in WWII.

De Havilland's Moths

Planes for the Proletariat

IN THE MID-1920S, there was a surge in the light plane movement, initially in the United Kingdom and Germany. Private flying in Germany, both of light aircraft and of gliders, was officially encouraged as efforts were made to circumvent the Versailles Treaty's restrictions on military flying. Many pilots of the future Luftwaffe gained their wings in a local flying club. Similar encouragement was offered in Britain, principally through the far-sighted efforts of Sir Sefton Brancker, the Director General of Civil Aviation. He saw that considerable benefits were to be had from making the average person more air-minded, not least because in any future war a nucleus of trained pilots would be invaluable. In 1924, a start was made when a scheme was announced that offered modest subsidies to selected flying clubs. The following year, that money helped to introduce the first of Geoffrey de Havilland's little Moths, aircraft that became a symbol of flying for pleasure. Francis Chichester described his delight in getting to know his D.H.60G Gipsy Moth: "The day arrives when at last you make two three-point landings in succession. It is the same as being in love; your heart swells with love for your neighbour...you forget your creditors, the world is at your feet, flying is child's play.... In short, complete happiness is your portion."

The first two-seat Moth was produced in 1925. It was both light and robust, and it was relatively cheap and easy to fly. It led the way toward a worldwide revolution in private flying. Together with its successors, particularly the D.H.82 Tiger Moth, de Havilland's biplane served as the backbone of the private flying movement in half the countries of the world between the wars and continued to be seen as the essence of flying for pure enjoyment for the rest of the century. The writer Roald Dahl learned to fly in a Tiger Moth, and loved the experience: "The Tiger Moth is a thing of great beauty. Everybody who has ever flown a Tiger Moth has fallen in love with it. You could throw one about all over the sky and nothing ever broke. You could glide it upside down hanging in your straps for minutes on end, and although the engine cut out when you did that because the carburettor was also upside down, the motor started at once when you turned her the right way up again. You could spin her vertically downwards for thousands of feet and then all she needed was a touch on the rudder-bar, a bit of throttle and the stick pushed forward and out she came in a couple of flips. A Tiger Moth had no vices. She never dropped a wing if you lost flying speed coming in to land, and she would suffer innumerable heavy landings from incompetent beginners without turning a hair."

Prominent among Moth aviators was Amy Johnson, an intensely independent woman who shared Amelia Earhart's determination to promote equality of the sexes. Johnson was the daughter of a fishmonger and earned her living as a typist. She was fascinated by aviation and spent her spare money on flying lessons. She also showed considerable technical aptitude, and was the first British woman to gain an aircraft ground engineer's certificate. She acquired her pilot's licence in 1929 and immediately began thinking of doing more than local flying. In 1930, she bought a de Havilland D.H.60G Gipsy Moth, powered by a 100-horsepower Gipsy

After only 85 hours of solo flying, a London secretary named Amy Johnson took off in a D.H. Gipsy Moth from London on May 5, 1930, in an attempt to break the record for flying from England to Australia. **Opposite:** Amy Johnson's Gipsy Moth, *Jason,* which today hangs in the London Science Museum's Flight gallery, is a small, unsophisticated aircraft, with a simple wood and fabric structure.

To the writer Roald Dahl, the de Havilland D.H.82 Tiger Moth was "a thing of great beauty." He added that "Everybody who has ever flown a Tiger Moth has fallen in love with it." The first D.H.82 was flown in 1931, and the type became the backbone of the private flying movement all over the world in the 1930s. More than 9,000 Tiger Moths were built, and over 1,000 of them were still being flown at the dawn of the 21st century. The aircraft seen here is flown by Clive Denny from the Imperial War Museum's airfield at Duxford, near Cambridge, England.

engine. She named her aircraft *Jason*. Inexperienced though she was, Amy Johnson promptly announced that she meant to fly this frail little biplane to Australia in an attempt to beat Bert Hinkler's record of fifteen days from London to Darwin.

With fewer then 100 logged hours, and flying the Moth for only the third time, Johnson took off from Croydon, near London, on May 5, 1930, heading for Vienna. Her departure attracted little attention, but by the time she reached Karachi she was two days ahead of Hinkler's time and was an overnight celebrity. From there, things did not go so well. In Burma, she damaged a wing landing on a sports field and had to improvise repairs with fabric strips torn from shirts. After a forced landing on Timor, ant hills

had to be leveled before she could take off again. *Jason* reached Port Darwin on May 24, nineteen and a half days after leaving London. Hinkler's record was intact, but Johnson's failure to beat his time was ignored by an ecstatic public. She had flown a light aircraft nearly 10,000 miles over some of the world's most rugged country and that was more than enough. That a young woman with Amy's humble background could bring off such a staggering achievement endeared her to people everywhere and brought her congratulations from kings and commoners all over the world. She wrote of her 10,000-mile flight: "The prospect did not frighten me, because I was so appallingly ignorant that I never realized in the least what I had taken on."

Left: In 1931, Francis Chichester fitted his D.H.60G Gipsy Moth *Mme Elijah* with floats for a crossing of the Tasman Sea that involved staging at two tiny islands. He adopted "deliberate error" navigation for the flight, a system that became generally accepted as the best method for finding small pieces of land in a vast ocean. **Below:** The D.H.87 Hornet Moth is one of Geoffrey de Havilland's delightful Moth family. First flown in 1934, in its original form it had tapered wingtips. These were modified to square after there were problems with tip stalling at slow speed. A total of 165 were built. This beautifully restored example is owned and flown in the United Kingdom by Mark Miller.

Waco

"Ask Any Pilot"

THE PERIOD BETWEEN THE world wars saw growing interest in personal aviation. The great number of WWI veterans who returned to the United States as qualified pilots fueled that increase in enthusiasm for private flying. In the first few years immediately after war's end, however, there were vast numbers of surplus machines available, and the general public still regarded flying as a dangerous pursuit reserved only for the foolhardy or intrepid. The booming economy of the 1920s and Lindbergh's Atlantic crossing in 1927 did much to increase public confidence and enthusiasm. By the mid 1920s, the quest to provide a relatively cheap and easy aircraft was on. In the United States there were many who felt they had the solution to aviation success. Existing firms expanded and new companies formed. The few that survived became the classics of aviation of the Golden Age. One of those manufacturers was the Weaver Aircraft Company, known far better for the acronym WACO (pronounced *waah-co*). Very much like the de Havilland Moth series in the United Kingdom, the Waco became the airplane of choice for American pilots of the era.

The Weaver Aircraft Company was founded in 1920 in Lorain, Ohio, by George "Buck" Weaver, a barnstormer, Elwood "Sam" Junkin, Clayton "Clayt" Bruckner and Charles "Charlie" William Meyers. Over the next 26 years, the Waco name would become synonymous with affordable and easy-to-fly aircraft. Weaver Aircraft moved to Troy, Ohio, in 1923, and the company name was changed to the Advance Aircraft Company although the aircraft retained the Waco designation. The company became a pioneer in the development and manufacture of small

Colonel Mackay's metalized Waco Taperwing on the grass at Troy, Ohio, Sky Harbor airstrip. **Opposite:** Waco Classic of Battle Creek, Michigan, is building new Waco YMF biplanes today from the original drawings approved in the 1930s. These wonderful aircraft bring back the gentle sound of radial engines to the skies of North America and the United Kingdom. One is flown here over a Michigan landscape of lakes and trees.

two- and three-seat passenger airplanes for private and commercial owners, beginning with the first Troy-built model in a long line of Waco aircraft, the Waco 6.

Waco's fabric-covered fuselage was constructed from welded-steel tubing, shaped with wooden formers and stringers. The wings were fabricated with spruce spars, spruce and wooden ribs, and aluminum leading edges. Linked ailerons on both wings provided positive and responsive control. The Waco earned a reputation for stable handling characteristics that made them forgiving craft without sacrificing good performance.

In early 1927, the company designed the Waco Model 10, which featured the first "oleo" strut, hydraulic, shock absorbing landing gear ever offered on a light commercial airplane. The Model 10 also offered more wing area, larger cockpits, an adjustable stabilizer, and, most important, an overall improvement in performance over the Model 9. The Waco 10 was offered with a variety of engines such as the OX-5, OXX-6, Hispano-Suiza and, late in 1927, the new Wright J-5 "Whirlwind" when it became available. In 1927 an OX-5 powered Waco 10 won the class B transcontinental New York to Spokane Air Derby, and in 1928 Whirlwind-powered Waco10s won many competitions including the prestigious National Air Tour. Waco continued to refine the aircraft design and accessories on an annual basis, but retained the basic configuration to maintain quality and avoid the high costs of wholesale redesign; as a result, selling prices remained stable and affordable.

The beautifully restored LINCO Waco Taperwing. BFGoodrich (now Goodrich Aircraft Wheels and Brakes) funded the restoration of this unique and historic aerobatic champion in the 1990s. This nimble and fun-to-fly Waco Taperwing was flown by Colonel Macky to win the International Aerobatic Championship in 1934. Today it is flown by airshow ace performer Bob Wagner, also from the Troy, Ohio, area.

What would become perhaps the most famous Waco, Model ATO *Taperwing* (S/N A118), was rolled out of the Waco Aircraft factory on July 8, 1929. In August of 1934, the aircraft was purchased by stunt pilot and skywriter Colonel Joseph C. Macky, who upgraded the aircraft to a Model CTO by installing a Wright Whirlwind R-975 J6-9 engine. In 1936, the *Taperwing* was completely reworked with streamlined fairing by Hill Aircraft of Cincinnati. It was the only Waco every metallized; the fuselage fabric skins were replaced with rounded aluminum skins.

Joe Macky established Macky Flying Service of Findlay, Ohio, and his team was contracted by the Ohio Oil Company (later Marathon Oil) to perform air shows, skywriting, and sign flying as the Linco Flying Aces. Asked to represent the United States at the 1936 International Air Games in Paris, Macky gave an incredible performance that earned him the Grand Prize Trophy, $10,000 and a hero's reputation and welcome across the globe. Macky went on to use this special Waco to earn many other awards for his aerobatic excellence, including the coveted Freddie Lund Trophy.

BFGoodrich acquired Colonel Macky's aircraft in 1993 and coordinated complete restoration of the *Taperwing*, bringing it back to flying condition. It is today flown from Waco Field in Troy, Ohio.

The jewel of Waco's efforts, and their last open-cockpit model for the barnstorming pilots of the 1930s, was the Waco YMF. Production of Waco civil aircraft was suspended in 1942 after the U.S. entry into World War II. The company contributed to the war effort by building assemblies for a variety of military aircraft and manufactured the widely used CG4-A Hadrian troop-carrying gliders used in Sicily, Normandy, the China-Burma theater and northern Europe. Waco ceased production in 1946, another victim of the postwar general aviation bust, but the brand still enjoys enormous popularity among aviation enthusiasts.

In 1983, Classic Aircraft Corporation in Battle Creek, Michigan, set out to recreate the classic YMF. While maintaining the sanctity of the design, the team modernized the aircraft with over 300 engineering changes, redrew over 1,400 drawings, and built new tooling for production. More than 5,000 hours of craftsmanship is dedicated to each new classic.

Flying wires and open cockpit: the pleasure of piloting a wonderful and reliable airplane through the summer skies is what flying is all about. The Waco line of aircraft, original, restored or new, remains the standard for classic private flying.

Lockheed Vega

Versatile Adventurer

THE ARCTIC WAS CROSSED by a heavier-than-air machine for the first time in 1928 by Australian adventurer Hubert Wilkins and his pilot, Carl Ben Eielson. Wilkins had seen the new Lockheed Vega on its maiden flight in California on July 4, 1927, and knew immediately that it was the aircraft for the boundless expanses of the Arctic. He ordered one and, painted bright orange and fitted with skis, it was flown to Point Barrow in March 1928. Wilkins and Eielson set out on their 2,200-mile flight to Spitsbergen on April 15. The Vega was in the air for over 20 hours before a storm forced a landing on a deserted island just 5 miles from the destination. Five days later, the storm abated and they were able to complete their epic journey. It was greeted with universal acclaim, and Amundsen went so far as to say: "No flight has been made anywhere, at any time, which could be compared with it."

After becoming the first woman to cross the Atlantic by air as a passenger in June 1928, Amelia Earhart said: "I do not believe that women lack the stamina to do a solo trip across the Atlantic." Four years later, she proved it. On May 20 and 21, 1932, Earhart flew a Lockheed Vega from Harbour Grace, Newfoundland to a Northern Ireland cow pasture in 14 hours, 54 minutes. Within three months she became the first woman to fly nonstop from Los Angeles to New York. She was rewarded for her achievements with the Gold Medal of the National Geographic Society and in the United States was voted Outstanding Woman of the Year. She came back into the headlines in 1935 with more long-distance flights in her Vega, becoming the first ever to fly from Hawaii to San Francisco and from Mexico City to New Jersey.

Adventurer Wiley Post standing in the cockpit on of his famous Lockheed Vega, *Winnie Mae*. **Opposite:** On display at the National Air & Space Museum, the Lockheed Vega that Amelia Earhart flew across the Atlantic Ocean in May of 1932, thus becoming the first woman to fly the Atlantic solo. The Vega had a novel design, with a monocoque fuselage and cantilever wing, which produced unusually high performance for the time.

An oilfield accident led to the loss of Wiley Post's left eye, but that did not prevent him from becoming one of the great names of aviation's golden years. As the personal pilot of oilman F.C. Hall, he flew a Lockheed Vega named after the oilman's daughter, *Winnie Mae*. Post believed that the aircraft could be used for setting aviation records. It particularly rankled with him that the fastest global circumnavigation had been accomplished by the *Graf Zeppelin* rather than a fixed-wing aircraft, so in 1930 he began planning to fly round the world. The *Winnie Mae* was modified with extra fuel tanks and improved instrumentation, and Australian Harold Gatty was engaged as the navigator.

Post and Gatty took off from Roosevelt Field, New York, on June 23, 1931, aiming to circle the globe via Berlin, Moscow, Novosibirsk, Irkutsk, Blagoveshchensk, Khabarovsk, Nome, Fairbanks, Edmonton and Cleveland. There were some disturbing incidents along the way. Taking off from a soft sand beach near Nome, the *Winnie Mae* nosed over and the propeller tips were bent. Post improvised a repair with a hammer, a wrench and a large rock and then ran the engine to test for vibration. Gatty, standing near the nose when Post cranked the engine, was struck on the shoulder by the propeller. Fortunately his injuries were no more than a severe bruise and a sprained back and they were able to continue. At Edmonton, the airfield was soggy from rain and Post was wary about taking off from another soft surface. In a remarkable gesture, the city authorities authorized him to use Edmonton's paved main street, and arranged for the removal of power and telephone lines to make it possible.

Slowed by these events and by a couple of brief unscheduled stops when they were uncertain of their position, Post and Gatty nevertheless had no difficulty in obliterating the *Graf Zeppelin*'s time, landing back at New York on July 1, 1931, eight days, 15 hours and 51 minutes after leaving. The *Winnie Mae* had spent just over 107 hours in the air while traveling 15,474 miles. Still not satisfied, Post, began to talk about the possibility of doing it all again — by himself.

Post took off on his solo flight from New York on July 15, 1933, and landed at Tempelhof, Berlin, 25 hours and 45 minutes later. He was the first to fly directly between the two cities. Delighted Germans offered him food and beer, but Post declined all hospitality and was on the ground for only two hours and 15 minutes. Fatigue now led to errors. He left his maps of the Soviet Union behind and had to land at Königsberg, East Prussia. There he discovered a leak in the autopilot's oil supply line and arranged to stop at Moscow for repairs. Distracted by the change in plans, he left Königsberg without his luggage. Other problems forced him

down at Irkutsk and again at Skovorodino, Siberia. Over Alaska, Post got lost and landed on a short dirt airstrip at the little town of Flat, where he ran into a ditch, damaged the right undercarriage leg and bent the propeller. All was not lost, however. Alaskan aviators came to Post's rescue, flying in a mechanic with a new propeller. By the time he had taken some much needed rest, the *Winnie Mae* was ready to go. Still very tired, on the leg from Edmonton to New York he dozed as the autopilot flew on. To prevent himself falling into a deep sleep, he held a wrench in his hand and tied it to one of his fingers. If he slept, the wrench fell and jerked him awake.

Fifty thousand people gathered at Floyd Bennett Field to welcome Wiley Post back to New York. When he touched down, the official timers of the National Aeronautic Association stopped their watches at seven days, 18 hours, forty-nine and a half minutes. He had beaten his previous global mark by more than 21 hours. Besides claiming a new round-the-world record, Post was the first to fly round the world twice and the first to do it alone.

Earhart's aircraft was a Lockheed Vega Model 5B powered by a Pratt & Whitney 450-horsepower Wasp engine. This reliable engine allowed her to cruise at 140 mph, and with it she covered the distance between Newfoundland and Ireland in just under 15 hours.

Top: In 1929 Roscoe Turner convinced Gilmore Oil to buy a Lockheed Air Express, *Black Hornet,* in which he set several transcontinental speed records, accompanied by a lion cub he acquired and named Gilmore. Above Left: Amelia Earhart is America's most famous woman aviator. She had many accomplishments, but is best remembered for two events: her solo crossing of the Atlantic in 1932 and her disappearance into the vast Pacific during an attempt to fly around the world in 1937. Above Right: This is a partial lineup of the competitors who flew the All-Women's Air Derby of 1929, photographed before the cross country race. Popularly called "The Powder Puff Derby," the race was flown between Santa Monica, California, and Cleveland, Ohio, and timed to reach the terminus during the Cleveland Air Races. Left to right: Louise Thaden, Bobbi Trout, Patty Willis (did not compete), Marvel Crosson (perished in crash), Blanche Noyes, Vera Dawn Walker, Amelia Earhart, Marjorie Crawford (did not compete), Ruth Elder, Florence "Pancho" Barnes.

Douglas DC-3

Legendary Workhorse

FEBRUARY 1933 SAW THE first flight of the Boeing 247 and from that moment all other passenger aircraft seemed obsolete. Apparently set to dominate the world of commercial aviation, the 247 in fact served merely as the catalyst for even greater things to come. United Air Lines, aware of the aircraft's potential from the design stage, ordered 60, a massive order that monopolized Boeing's production. United's forceful action had the unforeseen consequence of forcing TWA to seek new aircraft elsewhere. In August 1932, in a letter to Douglas Aircraft, TWA set out its requirements for a trimotor capable of carrying 12 passengers and cruising at 145 miles per hour over a 1,000-mile range. Douglas responded with a proposal for a twin-engined aircraft, noting that it would need to survive an engine failure on takeoff with a full load at any airport used by TWA. Acceptance of the proposal led to the DC-1, which first flew on July 1, 1933. It was a revelation, a truly modern airliner that more than matched the 247. In a proving flight across the continent, the DC-1 made it nonstop from Burbank, California, to New York in 11 hours, five minutes. With its fuselage stretched by two feet and seats for 14 passengers, it was produced as the DC-2, which dramatically confirmed its promise to the world when it won the handicap trophy and came second overall to the specially built D.H. Comet in the 1934 England-to-Australia air race, covering the 11,123 miles in three days, 18 hours and 17 minutes. Over 200 DC-2s were built and were operated by a variety of airlines, including TWA, American, Eastern and Pan American in the U.S., plus KLM, Iberia, Swissair and a number of others overseas.

Before the venerable Douglas DC-3 commanded the skies, the DC-1 and DC-2 proved the viability of the design. In a proving flight, the twin-engined DC-1 flew nonstop across the U.S. in 11 hours and 5 minutes. This DC-1 is wearing TWA colors. **Opposite:** A familiar sight at airports around the world, the Douglas DC-3. The wide stance of the undercarriage makes this aircraft able to operate from very rough and short airfields.

American Airlines then proposed a larger version of the DC-2, with room for 14 sleeping berths. Initially reluctant, Donald Douglas was persuaded by a promise for American to buy 20 aircraft. On July 8, 1935, American's president confirmed an initial order of ten Douglas Sleeper Transports at a cost of $79,500 each. So was born, almost by accident, the most celebrated transport of the piston-engined era. The DST first flew on a day heavy with significance in aviation history. It was December 17, 1935, 32 years after Kittyhawk. The DST entered transcontinental service as a sleeper in September 1936, but the Douglas assessment that the market for such an aircraft would be limited was correct and not many were built. However, with the berths removed, the fuselage could accommodate 21 seats, and a modified version appeared — the Douglas DC-3.

The DC-3 deserves to be regarded as one of the greatest aircraft ever produced. Initially fitted with 1000-horsepower Wright Cyclones, it was most often supplied with 1200-horsepower Pratt & Whitney Twin Wasps. These gave it a cruising speed of 170 miles per hour over an average stage length of 500 miles. Good figures though these were in the mid-1930s, the secrets of the DC-3's success and longevity lie in its sterling qualities as a transport aircraft. Pilots loved it for its forgiving nature, and engineers for the ease with which it was kept flying. Its reliability became legendary, and it was rugged enough to survive the punishment of operating from rough fields and in all kinds of weather. No aircraft, before or since, has matched the DC-3's adaptability — main-route airliner, feeder-liner, freighter, executive aircraft, and military jack-of-all-trades.

Above: The Army Air Forces military version of the DC-3 was designated C-47. General Eisenhower rated the C-47 one of the most indispensable tools that helped to win World War II. These reliable and adaptable cargo haulers were used in every theater of the war. This C-47 is on display at the National Museum of the USAF in Dayton, Ohio. **Left:** On June 6, 1944, American paratroopers jumped into occupied France and became the spearhead of the invasion now known as D-Day. Jack Reames of Vandalia, Ohio, was a member of the 82nd Airborne Division, 508th Parachute Infantry Regiment, C Company. He was 19 years old when he made his first combat jump — out of a C-47 into Normandy at 3:17 A.M. on D-Day.

From the beginning, the DC-3's potential was obvious and the Douglas factory was inundated with orders, with the U.S. military becoming the largest customer for a version designated C-47. By the time production stopped, a total of 17,299 DC-3s (and derivatives) had been produced; these included 10,654 built in the United States, 6,157 in the Soviet Union (Li-2s) and 487 in Japan. Their contributions during WWII were so substantial that General Eisenhower rated the C-47 as one of the four most significant items of war-winning equipment. They went on to fly on the Berlin Airlift and to see combat again in Korea and Vietnam, where they were in action as both transports and gunships. After WWII, large numbers of surplus C-47s were converted for civil use and operated into every corner of the globe, from the Arctic's icefields to the dirt strips of the Australian outback. On October 31, 1956, one U.S. Navy variant, an R-4D named *Que Sera Sera*, became the first aircraft ever to land at the South Pole. At one time or another, DC-3 types have been flown by almost all of the world's airlines and air forces, and it has proved impossible to replace them with a single type of such wide-ranging capability.

In 1936, President Franklin D. Roosevelt awarded the Collier Trophy to Donald Douglas for his achievements with the DC-3. Many examples were still flying more than 70 years after the DST's first flight. Few aircraft can lay claim to such an illustrious history.

Left: Martha Lunken, recently retired from the Federal Aviation Administration, is one of the few check pilots to qualify new DC-3 pilots in the U.S. She is seen here flying "The Goon" through the skies of Georgia in late summer 2005. **Above:** The DC-3's reputation and longevity had a lot to do with the very reliable Pratt & Whitney Twin Wasp 14-cylinder radial engines. No aircraft before or since has matched the DC-3's adaptability.

Short Brothers' Flying Boats

Imperial Flagships

IN JULY 1936, THE first Short S.23 "C" (Empire) class flying boat was launched, and on June 2, 1937, *Canopus* set off from Southampton to inaugurate the Imperial Airways service to Durban. ("C" class aircraft all had names beginning with C, including *Cavalier, Caledonia, Calpurnia, Cameronian, Capella, Caribou, Cassiopeia, Castor, Centaurus, Corinna, Coriolanus, Corsair and Cooee.*) From June 1937 onward, Empire boats were regularly employed over the routes between Southampton and both Durban and Sydney. Powered by four 920-horsepower Bristol Pegasus radials, they cruised at about 160 miles per hour and had a range of some 760 miles. On the Empire routes they usually carried some one and a half tons of freight and air mail, allowing room for only 17 passengers. These pampered few enjoyed first-class treatment, being accommodated in two spacious cabins plus a promenade cabin, and having separate lavatories for ladies and gentlemen. Food was produced in a large galley; pâté de foie gras, poached salmon, roast fillet of lamb, peach Melba, and crêpes Suzette were among the menu items, and they were accompanied by a selection of fine wines. Overnight stops were in five-star hotels. Even so, the journey could be something of a challenge, since the flying boats were noisy and could not fly high enough to avoid rough weather. They were, nevertheless, a considerable improvement on what had been before. Between mid-1938 and the outbreak of war in 1939, the Durban flight schedule was cut to only four and a half days, while Singapore was being reached in five and a half days, and Sydney in another four. For the privilege of beating the time of the fastest ocean liner by three weeks, a return

The Short 184 entered service in 1915, and soon proved a reliable performer. On August 12, 1915, during the Dardanelles campaign, a Short 184 became the first aircraft to sink a ship with a torpedo.
Opposite: The Short Sunderland was a vital element of RAF Coastal Command's war against the U-Boats in World War II. An evolution of the Empire class flying boats, the Sunderland had an endurance in excess of 13 hours.

fare from the United Kingdom to Australia cost £274 (then about $1,100), which in the 1930s would have bought a small house.

A remarkable experiment in high-speed air mail delivery was made between Britain and North America in 1938. The Short *Mercury-Maia* composite consisted of a large four-engined flying boat and a much smaller four-engined floatplane. The floatplane (*Mercury*), full of fuel and loaded with mail and newspapers, was carried into the air on the back of the flying boat (*Maia*). On July 21, 1938, *Mercury*, flown by Captain D.C.T. Bennett, was released off the Irish coast at Foynes and then flew 2,930 miles to Montreal in 20 hours, 20 minutes. *Mercury* later demonstrated the full extent of its capabilities by flying non-stop to the Orange River in southern Africa after being launched over Dundee, Scotland. The distance of 5,997.5 miles set a record for floatplanes that remained unbroken at the dawn of the 21st century.

A regular transatlantic service was inaugurated with "C" class flying boats on August 8, 1939, but the service was terminated after only eight flights because of the outbreak of World War II. The aircraft were used throughout the war, and several remained in operation until 1947, when they were finally withdrawn from service. By that time the 42 "C" class flying boats had flown almost 38 million miles, of which *Canopus*, the fleet flagship, had flown close to 2,800,000 miles. During their ten years of operation these dependable transports compiled an outstanding record of service and were instrumental in changing the character of commercial aviation.

The Imperial War Museum's Short Sunderland on display at the IWM Air Museum at Duxford, Cambridgeshire, U.K. It appears here in 1999, along with other notable WWII aircraft: the de Havilland Mosquito in the lower left, and looking across the broad wingspan of the Avro Lancaster.

While Short Brothers were developing the S.23, they also worked on a military variant designated S.25, which was named the Sunderland. The S.25 first flew on October 16, 1937, and the RAF received a Sunderland Mark I in June 1938 when the second production aircraft was flown to Singapore. By the outbreak of war in Europe in September 1939, RAF Coastal Command was operating 40 Sunderlands. In the critical early years of World War II, it was the best of the RAF's maritime patrol aircraft. However, it could operate only out to 600 miles from base and, without effective radar, its effectiveness was limited to daylight hours. A Royal Australian Air Force Sunderland achieved the type's first unassisted kill of a U-boat on July 17, 1940.

In December 1941, production began of a more effective Sunderland variant, the Mark III, with a reshaped hull, better armament and ASV (Anti-Surface Vessel) radar. By 1943, Sunderlands had the much improved ASV Mark III and were armed with powerful Torpex depth charges rather than ineffectual antisubmarine bombs. In the Bay of Biscay, on July 30, 1943, three German submarines were proceeding together on the surface when Royal Australian Air Force Sunderland "U" of 461 Squadron commanded by Flight Lieutenant Dudley Marrows arrived on the scene. Marrows reported that: "The Submarines were…putting up a formidable barrage of cannon and machine gunfire. I decided that the only thing to do was to go in as low as possible. We went in, jinking violently, with all 30 guns of the three submarines firing at us. Shrapnel was hitting the fuselage like hail. Just skimming the swell tops, I had to pull up to clear the submarine as I dropped my depth charges. We just cleared the conning tower." Seven explosions shredded U-461, literally blowing the U-boat apart. Flight Lieutenant Marrows saw survivors in the water, flew back and dropped a dinghy. Fifty-three of the U-boat crew died, but 15 survived.

On October 10, 1943, Dudley Marrows was awarded the Distinguished Flying Cross. This was followed up only three days later with the Distinguished Service Order. The awards were well deserved for what had been an intense action — and a bizarre coincidence. Of all the German submarines at sea on July 30, 1943, Sunderland "U" from 461 Squadron had engaged and destroyed U-461.

Michael Turner's painting of a Short Empire flying boat operating on Imperial Airways routes in the Far East. Empire boats were regularly employed over routes between Southampton to Durban and Sydney, Australia. Their 24 passengers were pampered with food produced in a large galley, and overnight stops were in five-star hotels. Even so, the journey could be something of a challenge, since the flying boats were quite noisy and could not fly high enough to avoid rough weather.

Messerschmitt Bf 109

Formidable Fighter

THE MESSERSCHMITT BF 109 WAS designed by Willy Messerschmitt in the early 1930s. With such features as all-metal monocoque construction, a closed canopy and retractable landing gear, it was a dramatic advance over the fighters of the biplane era. Early versions of the Bf 109 were combat tested with the Condor Legion during the Spanish Civil War, and when Germany attacked Poland on September 1, 1939, the Luftwaffe's principal fighter was the much improved and more heavily armed Messerschmitt Bf 109E.

After the fall of France in May 1940, the Bf 109E was heavily involved in the Battle of Britain. At the time it could claim to be as fast as the RAF's Spitfire and much faster than the Hurricane. Luftwaffe ace Heinz Lange was sure that his Bf 109 was "superior to the Hurricane and at least a match for the Spitfire." It was a steady gun platform and had the advantage of having armament that included a 20 mm cannon. The Daimler Benz DB 601 engine was fuel injected and would not cut out under negative G, unlike the carburetor-equipped Merlins of its RAF opponents. Effective though it was in the hands of seasoned pilots such as Adolf Galland and Werner Mölders, however, the Bf 109 had weaknesses. The cockpit was cramped and its canopy offered little headroom; the controls were not well harmonized and became extremely heavy as speed increased. Perhaps even worse was the narrow, spindly undercarriage, on which was laid the blame for more Bf 109s being damaged or destroyed in landing and taxiing accidents than in combat in the course of the war. An even more serious shortcoming was the limited fuel capacity, which allowed the Bf 109 only a few minutes of combat over London even when operating from bases near the French coast.

Willi Messerschmitt designed what would become one of the premier fighters of World War II, a streamlined single-seat fighter that evolved and was adapted to increasingly powerful engines. The Bf 109C here was sent to Spain and flown during the Spanish Civil War. **Opposite:** Bf 109G-2 *Black Six* warms up before takeoff.

The Battle of Britain resulted in the Luftwaffe being repulsed, with a loss of 1,733 aircraft to the defending RAF fighters. Although on the losing side, the Bf 109 nevertheless lived up to its reputation and proved itself in combat against well-trained and well-led opponents. The RAF's principal concern was to destroy bombers, and that meant running the gauntlet of escorting Luftwaffe fighters. The Bf 109s took good advantage of this and over 900 Spitfires and Hurricanes fell to their guns between July 10 and the end of October 1940.

Despite its shortcomings, the Bf 109 in its different versions remained a formidable fighter throughout the war. More kills were recorded by Bf 109 pilots than those flying any other aircraft, and at various times Bf 109s served as air superiority fighters, escort fighters, interceptors, ground-attack aircraft and reconnaissance aircraft. More Bf 109s were produced than any other combat aircraft, with over 31,000 built.

The Bf 109 was flown by such high-scoring aces as Erich "Bubi" Hartmann, the top-scoring fighter ace of all time (352 confirmed victories in 825 combat sorties) and Gunther Rall (275 in 621 sorties). Hartmann always tried to get extremely close to his enemy and fire one short burst. Then he would break off. Dogfighting, he said, was "dangerous and a waste of time." He described his technique as "See — Decide — Attack — Coffee Break." Rall saw most of his combat on the Eastern Front. It was often fierce and intense, with multiple sorties flown each day. Once, in responding to the question "How did you relieve battle stress when you were fighting on the eastern front?" his answer was "You know, there is not much to do when you live in a tent on

the Russian plains." Rall also commented that the guns of the later-model Bf 109s were tightly grouped around the nose. "This meant that there was not much spread of shot, so shooting had to be accurate, and preferably from very close." When asked if the nose grouping meant that the cockpit filled with smoke when the guns were fired, he replied "No — if you do it right, the other guy gets smoke in *his* cockpit!" Another

remarkably talented Bf 109 pilot was Hans-Joachim Marseille, who achieved 158 victories against Allied pilots in North Africa, including claims for 54 aircraft shot down in one month and 17 aircraft in a single day. All of the Bf 109 aces were confident that the fighter, modified by continual improvements, could at least hold its own against any Allied opponent throughout the war.

Above: *Black Six* backlit by the September sun over a Thames estuary. This fighter, captured in Libya during World War II and brought to the U.K. for evaluation, is now on display at the RAF Museum Hendon. **Opposite Top:** Leading fighter ace Gunther Rall, in the cockpit of the Bf 109 on display at the National Air & Space Museum. All of his 275 aerial victories were gained in Bf 109s. **Opposite Left:** Taking off from the Duxford airfield, a later version, a Bf 109G-10. This evolution of Messerschmitt's design had a taller fin that gave the pilot greater control on takeoff and landing. **Opposite Right:** The spiral-painted spinner of the Bf 109G-10, through which pokes the muzzle of its 30 mm cannon.

Hawker Hurricane

Eight-Gun Destroyer

IN JUNE 1936, THE NAME Hurricane was formally adopted for the Hawker Aircraft Company's new monoplane fighter. It was an appropriate choice for an aircraft that was to find itself repeatedly in the eye of World War II's most intense storms. Hurricanes were in the front line from the first day of the war to the last, fighting in every theater and in many different roles. Much-loved by their pilots, they were rugged, adaptable and maneuverable, and among the steadiest aerial gun platforms ever designed. Yet, despite their admirable qualities and the extent of their contribution to the eventual Allied victory, they have not always received the recognition they deserve. Perhaps not as photogenic as Supermarine's Spitfire, nor as menacing as the Messerschmitt Bf 109, and not as fast as either, the Hurricane has been too often characterized as a workhorse, a term which hints at its capacity to carry the weight of a battle but says little of its effectiveness in attack. The historical record tells a different story. The Hurricane would be better called a warhorse, an aerial Bucephalus upon whose efforts one of the most crucial victories in the history of human conflict was built. Without Hawker's resilient monoplane fighter, the Battle of Britain could not have been won, and the world would almost certainly have become a very different place.

The first flight of the Hurricane prototype, K5083, was from Brooklands on November 6, 1935, and in July 1936, K5083 made its public debut to great acclaim at the Hendon Air Display. The first production Hurricane (L1548) was delivered to 111 Squadron at RAF Northolt and the squadron was fully equipped early in 1938. The commanding officer, Squadron Leader John Gillan, then did a bit of flag-waving. On February 10, he set out to show

RAF Squadrons in North Africa used the Hurricane in the battles with Rommel's Afrika Corps. These saw action in the siege of Tobruk.
Opposite: Running up the powerful Rolls-Royce Merlin engine on the newly restored Hurricane on the grass airstrip at Hawker Restorations in Suffolk, U.K.

that the Hurricane had an impressive turn of speed by flying from Northolt to Turnhouse, near Edinburgh, a distance of 327 miles, in less than one hour. At first, it seemed unfortunate that he had chosen a day when an exceptionally strong northerly wind was blowing. Flying at full throttle all the way, he landed at Turnhouse well over an hour later, having averaged a less than notable 280 miles per hour. He had planned to return to base the following day, but it occurred to him that the wind could be an asset if he refueled and went back immediately. This he did, touching down at Northolt just 48 minutes after taking off. Ignoring the northbound half of his flight and the contribution of the helpful tailwind, the Air Ministry announced that the Hurricane had averaged 409 miles per hour from Edinburgh to London. The news raised a few German eyebrows and convinced most of the British public that the RAF had a 400-mph fighter. When his fellow pilots learned the facts of the matter, they nicknamed Gillan "Downwind," a burden he bore for the rest of his RAF career.

Generally speaking, the Hurricane was considered to be an easy aircraft to fly. Test pilot Roland "Bee" Beamont, who was posted to France to join 87 Squadron in October 1939, having accumulated a total of 130 flying hours, said: "To a newcomer the Hurricane was an immensely powerful but not very demanding aeroplane. Its wide track undercarriage, stable and responsive flying characteristics and reliable engine and hydraulic system resulted in a general atmosphere of confidence on the squadron, so that the newcomer had no reason to be apprehensive." Number 87 Squadron was one of those sent to France, and Beamont was soon in action. During an attack on a German bomber formation he was particularly

Dennis David, seen here in the Hurricane I at the RAF Museum, Hendon, was a pilot with 87 Squadron in the
Battles of France and Britain, scoring 21 aerial victories.

grateful for his fighter's turning abilities: "We closed in on the Dorniers and I hit one pretty hard. I suddenly noticed some stuff coming down past me like bright rain. It was tracer bullets. There was a Messerschmitt 110 very close, doing a tight attack on me from above. I didn't know what I was doing. I hadn't the slightest idea, except that I thought if I'm under fire from a fighter the thing to do was pull that aeroplane of mine into the tightest possible turn, which I did. I got a view of that 110 diving away out of sight."

After the fall of France came the Battle of Britain, and the RAF's Hurricane squadrons were at the heart of the struggle. Without Sydney Camm's warhorse, the Battle could not have been won. On average, Hurricanes formed two-thirds of the strength of Fighter Command throughout, and they accounted for a similar proportion of the 1,733 Luftwaffe aircraft destroyed. By October 30, 1940, there were 34 Hurricane squadrons on strength in Fighter Command, including one Canadian, two Czech and two Polish squadrons. Number 303 (Polish) Squadron had been declared operational in August and became the most successful RAF unit in the Battle, shooting down 127 Luftwaffe aircraft. Number 303's top-scoring pilot was in fact a Czech, Josef Frantisek, who was credited with 17 victories during the month of September. Killed in action on October 8, he was one of 267 Hurricane pilots to lose their lives in the Battle of Britain.

Dennis David of 87 Squadron fought through both the Battles of France and Britain, achieving 21 aerial victories. He survived the war unscathed, flying both Spitfires and Beaufighters on operations and rising to the rank of Group Captain. In his book, *Dennis "Hurricane" David,* he leaves no doubt of his respect and affection for the Hurricane: "I have waged a long campaign to get the Hurricane given its due as the major victor in the Battle of Britain," David writes. "Although today it is far less famous than the Spitfire, in fact, Hurricanes shot down more enemy aircraft than all the Spitfires, anti-aircraft and other aircraft combined." He also recalls conversations with former Luftwaffe bomber airmen in which they confided that "the Hurricane was the aircraft they dreaded."

Right: Billy Drake flew Hurricanes in the Battle of France and scored four aerial victories before being shot down. By 1943, he had raised his score to twenty-four and a half in the air and 13 more destroyed on the ground. **Below:** The Hurricane IIC of the RAF's Battle of Britain Memorial Flight, over the Lincolnshire landscape near its base at RAF Coningsby. The workhorse of the Battle was the Hurricane, which outnumbered the Spitfire by about two to one. Inferior to the Luftwaffe's Bf 109 in speed, acceleration and rate of climb, it could out-turn its opponent and was a good steady gun platform.

Supermarine Spitfire

Mitchell's Legacy

WHENEVER THE GREAT AIRCRAFT of aviation's first century are discussed, the name Spitfire is certain to be among those mentioned. Supermarine's splendid fighter would be remembered for the classical elegance of its lines, if for nothing else. With its slim fuselage set on gracefully curved elliptical wings, the Spitfire was a raving beauty from the start. There was more to it than that, however — much more. The attractive appearance of its airframe was matched by the Spitfire's remarkable performance and great potential for development. Upon its introduction to service, the Spitfire became the Royal Air Force's foremost fighter, and it retained its dominance in the RAF's front-line throughout the era of the piston-engined monoplane. More than 20,000 of all variants were built, and from its earliest days it came to be thought of as the fighter pilot's ideal, an irresistible combination of power, grace and combat effectiveness. Douglas Bader, the RAF's celebrated legless fighter leader, said of the Spitfire: "Here was the aeroplane par excellence…in fact, the aeroplane of one's dreams."

The Spitfire took on a wider significance, too. For the British people in the dark early days of World War II, the aircraft and its name acquired an almost mystic quality. Although not then the RAF's most numerous fighter, the Spitfire caught the public imagination like no other instrument of war and became a symbol of the nation's defiance, a standard bearer pointing the way to eventual victory.

The Spitfire was born in the mind of a uniquely talented engineer. Reginald Mitchell was appointed chief designer of the Supermarine Aviation Works in 1919, when he was only 24. During the 1920s, he was principally involved with the design of marine aircraft of one

Two Spitfires from 616 Squadron, Mark Is, on final approach to landing, undercarriage and flaps down. The squadron badge is a Yorkshire rose, and the motto is "no rose without a thorn."
Opposite: A Mark Vb Spitfire flown by the Battle of Britain Memorial Flight taxis along the grass at the Audley End airstrip.

kind or another. His S.5, S.6, and S.6B floatplanes won the Schneider Trophy races in 1927, 1929 and 1931, and the S.6B became the first aircraft to achieve speeds above 400 miles per hour when it set a world air speed record of 407 miles per hour. Mitchell learned a lot about the problems of high-speed flight from the Schneider Trophy experience, and that hard-won knowledge was of great value when, in the early 1930s, he conceived the design of the monoplane fighter that became the Spitfire. He was already seriously ill with cancer, but he ignored his illness to concentrate on his work. After one particularly debilitating operation, he was forced to convalesce in Switzerland. He traveled through Germany where he saw something of the Luftwaffe's rising power. Aware that Germany was already better prepared for war than Britain, he redoubled his efforts on his return to the United Kingdom.

The first flight of Mitchell's prototype fighter (K5054) took place in March 1936. In the months that followed, a level true speed of 349 miles per hour at 16,800 feet was recorded and the limiting indicated airspeed of 380 miles per hour was reached in a dive. A height of 34,700 feet was achieved. While his creation went from strength to strength, Mitchell waned visibly. He was suffering from an incurable cancer and it had reached an advanced stage. He did not allow his deteriorating health to deter him. He still visited the factory or went to see the aircraft whenever he could, and his spirit seemed undimmed. A typically forthright comment burst out of him when he heard that the Air Ministry had accepted the name Spitfire for the fighter: "Spitfire! It's the sort of bloody silly name they would give it." On

Above: An immaculately restored Spitfire Mark XI flown by Clive Denney over the fields of Kent along the southeastern coast of the United Kingdom. The Mark IX was a wartime progression of the fighter that flew and fought the Battle of Britain. As the opposition aircraft became more powerful and developed greater firepower, the Spitfire also evolved in a deadly dance of advances in war and technology.

Right: Ray Hanna, founder of the Old Flying Machine Company, based at the Imperial War Museum's airfield at Duxford. Ray was the leader of the RAF Aerial Demonstration Team, the Red Arrows. The OFMC often provides restored aircraft for Hollywood film productions. One fine summer evening during the filming of *Memphis Belle,* Ray performed an "air test" of the Mark IX Spitfire he flies. As author Ron Dick recalls, "There were just a few of us sitting on the grass at Duxford enjoying a beer after a day's filming, when Ray disappeared. Soon you could hear the snarl of a Merlin coughing to life, and Ray taxied the Spitfire past us and took off. The next ten minutes or so, we were treated to an airshow just for us: Ray really wringing out the fighter. He landed it gently on the grass and taxied close to where we were sitting in the grass. He shut down the engine, and climbed out. With the motor still ticking and popping as it cooled, Ray sat down, picked up a beer and smiled at us. Wow!"

June 11, 1937, at the age of 42, Reginald Mitchell died, having seen to it that his aircraft was well established on the road to success. It was a legacy for which his country would have cause to be for ever grateful.

Al Deere, the indestructible New Zealander who flew the Spitfire and included three Bf 109s among his Battle of Britain victories, had no doubts about which was the superior aircraft. He wrote: "As a result of my prolonged fight with a 109, it was possible to assess the relative performance of the two aircraft. In early engagements…the speed and climb of the 109 had become legendary and were claimed by many to be far superior to the Spitfire. I was able to refute this contention and indeed was confident that, except in a dive, the Spitfire was superior in most fields and, like the Hurricane, vastly more maneuverable…. There were those who frankly disbelieved my claim, saying that it was contrary to published performance figures. Later events, however, proved me right."

The Mark II Spitfire flown by the Battle of Britain Memorial Flight is the world's oldest flying Spitfire. It saw action in the Battle of Britain, survived the war at a gunnery school, and was restored to flying condition in 1967 for the movie *The Battle of Britain*.

Boeing B-17

The Flying Fortress

THE BOEING B-17 DID not get off to a promising start. Having stolen the show with the B-17 prototype (Model 299) in a competition to provide a new bomber for the U.S. Army Air Corps, Boeing faced disaster. On October 30, 1935, the 299 crashed just after takeoff. The controls locks had been left engaged. Boeing's hopes went up in smoke, and the Douglas DB-1 (B-18) was declared the winner by default. The Air Corps, however, had been impressed by the 299. Approval was given for the acquisition of 13 aircraft for evaluation, plus one more for static tests. It was at this time that the new bomber acquired its name. A Seattle reporter was so amazed by a bomber with five gun positions that he called it "a Flying Fortress." Bitter experience in combat would later reveal that the name was an exaggeration of the truth, but it had a good sound and it stuck.

Keen to make their case for the B-17, the airmen flew over a number of cities in formation, after which their speeds between cities were always released for publication. In January 1938, Colonel Robert Olds broke the U.S. transcontinental record by flying from Langley, Virginia, to March Field, California in 12 hours, 50 minutes, and then flew back again in 10 hours, 46 minutes. Two goodwill tours of South America were completed without serious incident in a blaze of favorable publicity. Even so, the Secretary of War insisted there was no requirement for four-engined bombardment aircraft.

Complicating the issue was the antagonism of the U.S. Navy. In May 1938 the Air Corps used the Italian transatlantic liner *Rex* to represent an enemy fleet. In breach of the 1931 interservice agreement concerning air operations more than 100 miles from the coast, three B-17s set off from Mitchel Field, New York, to intercept the *Rex* some 700 miles out. The weather was bad, but the B-17s found the ship. The achievement was on the front pages of newspapers all across the United States. Claiming that the flight had been routine for B-17 crews, the airmen were unprepared for the U.S. Navy's protest about Army aircraft usurping blue water prerogatives. An embarrassed Army Chief of Staff sent down a verbal order restricting Air Corps activities to within 100 miles of the U.S. shoreline. The order was never formally issued, and therefore never properly rescinded, and its effects bedeviled Army aviation for many months.

Despite these various problems, the B-17 was ordered into production, but improved by major modification before the United States entered the war in December 1941. In 1942, B-17Es of the 97th Bomb Group were deployed to the United Kingdom to serve in the Eighth Air Force and they flew their first operational mission on August 17, 12 aircraft attacking marshaling yards at Rouen, France. Opposition was light and the bombing from 23,000 feet reasonably accurate. The raid boosted American morale considerably, but it was no harbinger of the struggles to come. Within a month, Luftwaffe fighters were pressing home their attacks and Eighth Air Force bomber losses began to mount. They reached 3.7 percent in November and climbed to a disturbing 8.7 percent in January 1943. Notable losses were suffered on June 13, 1943 (22 B-17s of 60 attacking Kiel), July 25 (15 of 100 against Hamburg), and August 12 (23 of 133 over the

As B-17s from the 390th Bomb Group return from a mission over occupied Europe, a mechanic pays attention to the Number 2 Wright-Cyclone radial engine. This is just one of the bombers he has to keep flying. **Opposite:** Engines Number 3 and 4 seen from the navigator's starboard window of Flying Fortress *Sentimental Journey*. Her companion B-17, *Texas Raiders,* is just off the wing in formation. These bombers are restored and operated by the Commemorative Air Force (formerly the Confederate Air Force).

Boeing B-17G *Shoo Shoo Baby* on the ramp at Wright Field in Dayton, Ohio. This restored B-17 was flown to the National Museum of the USAF in October of 1988, after a ten-year restoration project conducted by volunteers at Dover AFB in Delaware. This B-17 is a surviving combat veteran, flying 22 missions before it was flown to Sweden in May of 1944, after it suffered severe combat damage on a mission to Poznan, Poland. The crew was interned and the bomber survived after being used as an airliner by Sweden and an aerial mapping platform in France. *Shoo Shoo Baby* was found derelict on an airfield in France by aviation historian Steve Birdsall.

Ruhr). Even worse were the raids on Schweinfurt and Regensburg on August 17 (361 B-17s) and Schweinfurt again (291) on October 14. On each occasion, 60 B-17s were shot down, and the majority of the survivors returned with battle damage; many of them never flew again. Over Germany, the Luftwaffe was consistently imposing losses of well above 10 percent on the bombing force, a rate that would lead inexorably to its destruction. It was ever more apparent that the daylight bombing offensive could not be continued in the absence of escort fighters with the range to accompany the bombers over Germany.

The tide began to turn when P-51 Mustangs first began escorting the bombers in December 1943. By February 1944, they were making their presence felt in combat against the Luftwaffe deep inside Germany. At the same time, it became possible for the Eighth Air Force to launch over 1,000 bombers on missions in one day. Between February 20 and 25 ("Big Week"), over 3,300 Eighth Air Force bomber sorties pounded Germany's aviation industry. One of three Medals of Honor awarded to B-17 crew members on the first day of "Big Week" went to 1st Lieutenant Bill Lawley, a pilot from the 305th Bomber Group. Cannon shells set an engine on fire and shattered the cockpit, killing the copilot and wounding eight others. Lawley, bleeding profusely, held the dead copilot off the controls with one hand and recovered from a steep dive with the other. Electing not to bail out because of the injuries to his crew, Lawley endured another fighter attack en route to England that set fire to a second engine. Over southern England a third engine died, but Lawley, recovering from a temporary collapse caused by shock and loss of blood, managed to belly-land the B-17 on a grass airfield south of London, without further injury to his crew.

As the final bomber offensive gathered pace, the statistics told their own story — one bomber lost from 1,094 sent to Kassel, and none of 1,219 at Nurnburg. The B-17 force of the Eighth had grown to 106 squadrons by the end of WWII, and more than 291,000 sorties had been flown over Europe. There had been 640,000 tons of bombs dropped and 6,700 fighters claimed as destroyed. The number of B-17s of all models built was 12,731. Of these, 4,750, nearly 40 percent, were lost during operations. When training accidents and midair collisions are added, the total number of B-17s lost rises to over 8,000, nearly two-thirds of those built.

Flying into the sunset in Dave Tallichet's B-17. Silhouetted by the late afternoon sun are the bombardier's position and his weapon, the Norden bombsight. The grips of the .50-caliber machine gun are just to the right. Tallichet flew for the 100th Bomb Group, Eighth Air Force, and is the only owner and operator of a Flying Fortress to have flown one in combat and now on the airshow circuit. His brother-in-law was William Wyler, the great Hollywood director, who made the documentary *Memphis Belle* during the war. Catherine Wyler, daughter of the director, produced the late 1990s film *Memphis Belle,* and this B-17 is featured in the film as the "Belle."
Left: Harry Crosby was a lead navigator for the 100th Bomb Group. He wrote the classic book *A Wing and a Prayer,* about the experiences of the Eighth Air Force and the crewmen who flew and fought from B-17s in the early days of the bomber offensive against Nazi Germany.

Junkers Ju 52

Iron Annie

THE JUNKERS JU 52/3M WAS a very successful transport, but its boxy, corrugated fuselage denied it the aesthetic appeal of an aircraft like the Douglas DC-3. This rugged, essentially practical machine was manufactured from 1932 to 1945, and close to 5,000 were built to see both civilian and military service. It was a workmanlike design initially powered by three 525-horsepower BMW Hornets. In its civilian role, the Ju 52/3m flew as an airliner and freight hauler with more than a dozen air carriers, notably Lufthansa and Swissair. As an airliner, it carried 17 passengers, cruising at 150 miles per hour over ranges up to 500 miles. Some 75 percent of Lufthansa's European traffic went by Ju 52/3m in the 1930s. It was also the Luftwaffe's principal troop transport, occasionally pressed into service as a makeshift bomber, for instance during the bombing of Guernica during the Spanish Civil War and Warsaw in the early days of World War II. There was a floatplane version that served during the Norwegian Campaign in 1940 and later in the Mediterranean, some fitted with a large degaussing ring under the airframe for use as minesweepers.

Before WW II, the Junkers Ju 52 saw service throughout Europe. The reliable airliner and freight hauler made its debut in 1932.
Opposite: This example of the mainstay of the Luftwaffe's transport capabilities is on display at the National Museum of the USAF. Hitler was encouraged by the ease with which his neighbours were intimidated by "a few Ju 52s from Lufthansa and not even enough bombs for them."

Iron Annie made her first real impact on world affairs in 1936, when Hitler responded to General Franco's plea for help at the outset of the Spanish Civil War. Twenty Junkers Ju 52/3ms flew repeated shuttle trips across the Straits of Gibraltar, delivering nearly 14,000 troops from North Africa to Spain during the first three weeks of August 1936. It was the first major airlift of troops ever attempted, and, since the Nationalist cause could hardly have prospered without them, it was arguably the most decisive single operation of the war. Not for the last time, air transport units, perhaps lacking the glamorous public appeal of front-line combat squadrons, demonstrated the crucial importance of their role in military aviation.

In WWII, Ju 52/3ms were heavily involved from the beginning. During the Norwegian campaign in 1940, 580 of the transports flew over 3,000 sorties to deliver 29,280 men, 259,300 gallons of fuel and 2,376 tons of supplies. For the Battle of Crete in May 1941, some 500 Ju 52/3ms launched the largest German airborne operation of the war, dropping over 8,000 paratroopers on the island. Afterward, Crete was known as the graveyard of the *fallschirmjager* (paratroops); they lost nearly 4,000 men in the assault. The survivors hung on while Ju 52/3ms returned to land reinforcements behind them, eventually delivering some 30,000 men. The huge losses suffered by the paratroopers and the transports (170 Ju 52/3ms shot down) shocked the German High Command and large-scale airborne assaults were never again authorized by Hitler.

In February 1942, the Soviet Army surrounded 100,000 German soldiers around the town of Demyansk, northwest of Moscow. This initiated the first major rescue airlift in history on February 20, when Ju 52/3ms began flying into Demyansk in a continuous stream. Day after day, in all weathers and in the face of heavy antiaircraft fire and Soviet fighters, the transports kept coming. The siege was broken on May 18, by which time Iron Annies had flown more than 33,000 sorties, delivering 30,500 reinforcements and 64,844 tons of supplies, and taking out 25,400 casualties. It was a staggering performance, but it cost 265 transports, a force the Luftwaffe could ill afford to lose.

Above: This flying example of the Junkers transport is operated by the Great Lakes Wing of the Commemorative Air Force. It was built under license in Spain in the early 1950s. **Opposite:** The corrugated skin of this and many other large Junkers made them rugged and durable. Ju 52s were flown by the Luftwaffe into and out of Stalingrad, across the Mediterranean and in every theater of the war. In arguably the most decisive single operation of the Spanish Civil War, 20 Ju 52/3ms were sent across the Straits of Gibraltar in response to General Franco's appeals to Hitler and Mussolini for aircraft, The Luftwaffe moved nearly 14,000 troops and their equipment from Morocco to Spain in repeated shuttles over three weeks in August 1936.

It also gave the German High Command the false impression that a surrounded force could always rely on being supplied by air.

In November 1942, the Soviets succeeded in encircling the German 6th Army (over 250,000 men under General Paulus) at Stalingrad. The successful airlift at Demyansk encouraged Hitler to order Paulus to stand fast, and when the head of the Luftwaffe, Jeschonnek, assured the Führer that the 6th Army could be supplied by an "air bridge," the Luftwaffe was committed to a hopeless task. Paulus needed about 750 tons of supplies per day, which meant that 375 Ju 52/3ms had to land in the pocket every 24 hours. Even in good weather, this was far beyond the Luftwaffe's capabilities. Given a normal availability rate of only 35 percent, a huge force of over 1,000 transport aircraft would have had to be assembled. Even though other fronts were denuded of Ju 52/3ms to cope with the emergency, and some other aircraft were added to the fleet, the task was beyond them. Transports flying through winter storms to reach the pocket had to run the gauntlet of Soviet fighters and cross an increasingly dense belt of antiaircraft guns. Accidents were frequent, brought on by the appalling conditions

or by aircrew fatigue. Through December 1942 and January 1943 the best efforts of the Luftwaffe averaged a daily delivery of less than 100 tons to the besieged Germans. At the end of January, with the last of his airstrips overrun, the recently promoted Field Marshal Paulus surrendered. Only 90,000 of his men survived the siege to be taken prisoner and not more than 5,000 of those ever returned to Germany.

The defeat suffered by the Wehrmacht at Stalingrad was grievous, but the impact of the struggle on the Luftwaffe was no less devastating. The loss of over 700 aircraft included 269 Ju 52/3ms. As important as the material loss was the effect that the crew losses had on other parts of the Luftwaffe. Many of the airmen who flew into Stalingrad were on temporary detachment from their normal duties, notably as instructors, and their loss caused crew shortages and disruption in training programs which were not easily overcome.

Most of the surviving Ju 52/3ms were destroyed after WWII but some remained in service with the Swiss Air Force as late as the 1980s and several are still in regular use as flying museum pieces.

Mitsubishi A6M

The Zero

THE JAPANESE AIR FORCES were a revelation to their opponents. Their aircrew were well trained, their tactics were sound and their aircraft were formidable. The Zero fighter in particular quickly showed that it could outfly anything the Allied air forces had. First blooded over China in 1940, the Mitsubishi A6M, Type 0, known as the Zero, should not have come as a surprise to the Allies, but early reports of its performance were treated with skepticism and generally disbelieved. In fact, it was a remarkable fighter. Powered by a 950-horsepower radial engine, the Zero had a maximum speed of 330 miles per hour, which was slower than some of its competitors, but it had an excellent rate of climb and was incredibly maneuverable. Saburo Sakai, the Japanese ace who scored 64 victories in Zeros, described it as being "a dream to fly. The airplane was the most sensitive I had ever flown, and even slight finger pressure brought instant response." Its range, too, was extraordinary — nearly 2,000 miles with a drop tank — allowing Zeros to appear in areas thought to be unreachable by Japanese fighters.

A wartime photo of Horikoshi Jiro's famous fighter. This is an A6M2 Model 21 of the 3rd Kokutai at Rabaul in September of 1942. The designer of the Zero responded to Japanese pilots' "figurative demand for the blades and arts of the old masters." **Opposite:** This Nakajima-built A6M2 at the National Museum of the USAF. Found in Papua, New Guinea, it was probably one of the aircraft delivered to Rabaul and operated at Kavieng by the 6th and later 253rd Kokutai (Squadron).

Such outstanding performance came at a price, however. It was largely achieved by keeping the weight of the Zero as low as possible, not much more than 5,000 pounds fully loaded. Japanese fighter pilots were specific in demanding that their aircraft not be encumbered with what they regarded as excessive weight. Above all, they wanted a light, agile aircraft, comparing their fighters with "master craftsmen's Samurai swords." The designer of the Zero, Horikoshi Jiro, later wrote: "As a result of our pilots' figurative demand for the blades and the arts of the old masters, the Japanese fighters were the lightest in weight and among the most maneuverable in the world." Armor plate was not used, nor were

self-sealing fuel tanks. Once U.S. fighter pilots learned to use the superior speed and diving ability of their aircraft to advantage, and to avoid being drawn into low-speed turning dogfights, these shortcomings of the Zero were often brutally exposed.

One of the greatest Zero pilots was Saburo Sakai. On December 8, 1941, Sakai was the pilot of one of 45 Zeros in the force that attacked Clark airfield in the Philippines. In his first combat against Americans, he shot down a P-40, and then on December 10 he shot down a B-17 that was flown by Captain Colin P. Kelly. This was the first B-17 shot down during the war. Early in 1942, Sakai was transferred to Tarakan in Borneo. Japanese higher command had instructed fighter patrols to down any enemy aircraft encountered over the Dutch East Indies, whether they were armed or not. Just after shooting down one aircraft over Java, Sakai saw a civilian Dutch DC-3 at low altitude over the jungle. Sakai closed on the transport and noticed a blonde woman with a young child at one of the windows. The woman reminded him of a Mrs. Martin, an American who had occasionally taught him as a child in middle school. He decided, against his orders, not to shoot down the Dutch aircraft and signaled the pilot to fly on.

In April 1942, Sakai joined the Tainan Air Group at Lae, New Guinea. It was here over the next four months that he scored the majority of his estimated 64 aerial victories in battles with American and Australian pilots based at Port Moresby. His squadron included fellow aces Hiroyoshi Nishizawa and Toshio Ohta. After one mission attacking Port Moresby with 18 Zeros, these three were sufficiently sure of themselves to give a demonstration of formation aerobatics over the Allied air base.

On August 3, Sakai's air group was deployed from Lae to Rabaul. During a mission over Guadalcanal, Sakai made an almost fatal mistake. Thinking he was diving on an F4F Wildcat, Sakai attacked an SBD dive-bomber flown by Ensign Robert C. Shaw from Bombing Squadron Six (VB-6) aboard the USS *Enterprise*. A burst from the SBD's rear gunner, Harold L. Jones, shattered the canopy of the Zero. Sakai was struck in the head by a bullet, which blinded him in the right eye and paralyzed his left arm. The badly damaged Zero rolled over and headed seaward. Although in agony from his injuries, blind in one eye and bleeding profusely, Sakai managed to recover the Zero from its dive and, in one of the epic feats of endurance in WWII, fly it back to his base on Rabaul. It was a 560-nautical-mile flight and it took him four hours and 47 minutes. With the fuel gauge reading empty, he succeeded in landing the Zero without further damage, and insisted on reporting to his superior officer before he collapsed. Sakai was evacuated to Japan on August 12, where he endured surgery without anesthesia. The operation repaired some of the damage to his head, but was unable to restore full vision to his right eye. He returned to combat in 1944, and on June 24 approached a formation of fifteen aircraft that he thought were Japanese, but were actually U.S. Navy Hellcats. In the ensuing dogfight, Sakai proved that he had not lost his flying skill, despite the loss of one eye. Sakai eluded the Hellcats for over 20 minutes and returned to his airfield unscathed.

Above: The Misubishi A6M, Type 0, known as the Zero, was incredibly maneuverable. The nimble fighter is painted to represent a section leader's aircraft from the aircraft carrier *Zuiho* during the Battle of the Bismarck Sea, March 1943.
Right: Another example of the A6M exhibited at the National Museum of Naval Aviation in Pensacola, Florida. It is seen here nose to nose with its opposition from the early stages of the Pacific air war — the Grumman F4F Wildcat.

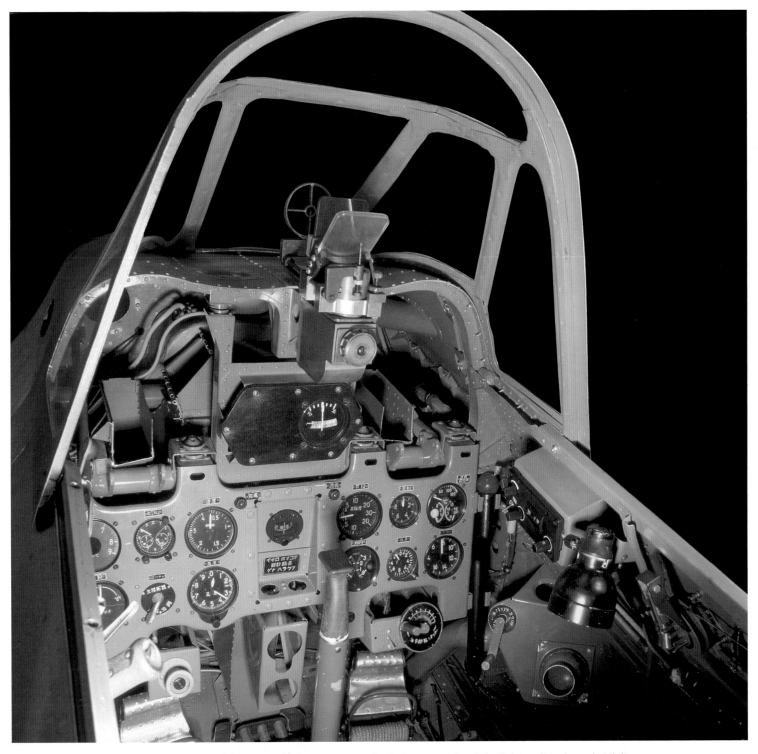

The roomy cockpit of the A6M. The instruments are logically arranged and the fighter offered good visibility.
The open trays on either side of the gunsight would have held the two forward-firing machine guns.

Avro Lancaster

Bludgeon and Rapier

BY THE TIME NAZI GERMANY was bludgeoned to defeat in 1945, Bomber Command of the Royal Air Force had evolved into an awesome instrument of destruction. Its capacity to wreak havoc on an opposing nation was formidable, and there was no doubt that its aircrews and their aircraft had played a significant part in bringing the Third Reich to its knees. Bomber Command's principal weapon for the assault was the Lancaster, an aircraft of which interwar air power theorists must have dreamed. In 1945, the Lancaster, with its huge bomb-bay and its acquired array of electronic devices, was indeed a bomber to be feared, but the path to its development had been long and painful, marked as it was by both political struggle and lack of military understanding.

The first flight of the Lancaster prototype (then still referred to as the Manchester III, a development of the failed Manchester I) took place on January 9, 1941. RAF bomber squadrons began to equip with Rolls-Royce Merlin-engined Lancaster Mk. Is in early 1942 and first used them operationally on March 10 against targets in Essen. More than 7,300 Lancasters were produced, Mks. I to VII in Britain and Mk. Xs in Canada. At the end of the war Lancasters were being operated by 56 front-line bomber squadrons.

The Lancaster was regarded with affection by its crews because it was rugged enough to survive considerable battle damage and still flew quite well on two engines. Although the controls were relatively heavy, the Lancaster was lively performer and could be thrown around in the corkscrew evasive maneuver, a disorientating sequence of steep wing-overs, rapid descents and high-G pull-outs. Many Lancaster crews came

Lancaster servicing was carried out by ground crew in the open air, summer or winter. **Opposite:** The Lancaster was the RAF's principal weapon in the bomber offensive against Germany. It had a cruising speed of 216 miles per hour at 20,000 feet while carrying 14,000 pounds of bombs. This is *Just Jane,* on display at the Lincolnshire Aviation Heritage Center in England.

back to attest to the corkscrew's effectiveness in shaking off attacks by Luftwaffe night-fighters.

The heart of the Lancaster was its exceptionally capacious bomb-bay. Until the much later Boeing B-29, an aircraft almost twice the Lancaster's size, no other wartime aircraft could approach the Lancaster in bomb-carrying capacity, and it was the only bomber to drop the 22,000-pound Grand Slam. A standard load for a Lancaster was 12,000 pounds, usually combining a single 4,000-pound Blockbuster and an assortment of 1,000-, 500- or 250-pound bombs, together with a number of 250-pound containers carrying incendiaries.

A study completed as early as 1943 noted that 132 tons of bombs were dropped for each Lancaster lost on operations. This compared very favorably with tonnages for the Halifax and Stirling, which were 56 and 41 respectively. By the end of the war, Lancasters had flown more than 156,000 operational sorties and dropped over 608,000 tons of bombs. (As a comparison, the B-17s and B-24s of the Eighth Air Force together flew some 295,000 sorties in dropping 641,000 tons.)

Although Lancasters were primarily associated with large night operations against German cities, they were used on occasion for precision attacks conducted at low-level. On April 17, 1942, a force of 12 Lancasters struck the MAN submarine diesel engine factory at Augsburg in southern Germany, a target 500 miles deep in enemy territory. Some damage was done to the factory, but the cost was horrifying. Seven of the 12 aircraft were shot down, four by fighters on the way to Augsburg and the others by flak in the target area. All of the returning Lancasters were heavily damaged by

flak. The raid leader, Squadron Leader J.D. Nettleton, survived the raid and was awarded the Victoria Cross. Despite the forbidding example of Augsburg, the experiment of conducting daylight low-level operations with unescorted heavy bombers was repeated six months later when 94 Lancasters attacked the Le Creusot armament works in France. This time, evasive routing over the Bay of Biscay helped in achieving complete surprise. The force was not intercepted and the only loss occurred when a Lancaster of 61 Squadron bombed Le Creusot power station at such a low level that it struck a building. That the force had indeed been flying at very low altitudes was confirmed by the post-raid remarks of one crew member who reported that the railway lines in France looked rusty, and another who thought the cows were underfed.

The most celebrated of the precision raids was flown against the Ruhr dams in May 1943. An elite unit was formed for this raid, 617 Squadron commanded by Wing Commander Guy Gibson, and a cylindrical "bouncing bomb" weighing 9,250 pounds was designed by Dr. Barnes Wallis. Nineteen modified Lancasters took off from RAF Scampton on the evening of May 16, 1943, to attack the Mohne, Eder and Sorpe dams. The attacks had to be made

from only 60 feet at exactly 240 miles per hour. The precise height was judged by the coincidence of two spotlights shining on the surface, and the correct range by lining up two uprights of a homemade bombsight with the towers at each end of the dams. It took four bombs to destroy the Mohne Dam and two more to ruin the Eder. The Sorpe, an earth-core dam, resisted the one bomb it received. Eight of the 617 Squadron crews were lost — four were shot down by flak, two hit power cables, one ran into a tree, and one was destroyed when the bomb struck the top of the dam wall and exploded under the aircraft. The raid was immensely destructive to the areas downstream of the dams, but it failed to achieve its object of denying water to the Ruhr industries. The Sorpe's survival ensured that just enough water was retained to keep things going until the other dams were repaired. Nevertheless, from an operational point of view, it was a tour de force, and Gibson was awarded the Victoria Cross for his inspired leadership. Targets impervious to conventional attack had been destroyed in a demonstration of accurate flying and precision bombing unequaled in WWII. It had been shown that the crushing bludgeon of the Lancaster could, when necessary, become a deadly rapier.

One of two Lancasters still in flying condition is operated by the Canadian Warplane Heritage Museum at Hamilton, Ontario. The aircraft is the Mynarski Memorial Lancaster, named in honor of Pilot Officer Andrew Charles Mynarski, who was posthumously awarded the Victoria Cross for his efforts to save a trapped crewmember from a burning Lancaster. Here museum members pose in authentic WWII bomber aircrew dress.

The approach to enemy airspace was invariably hazardous, as the crew of a 61 Squadron Lancaster found out on their way to Dusseldorf on November 3, 1943. At 21,000 feet, with the Dutch coast in sight, a Messerschmitt 110 hit them hard, its cannon shells ripping through the aircraft from end to end, damaging the elevator, both turrets, and the hydraulic system. The compass was among the instruments out of action and the canopy was shattered. The Scots captain, Flight Lieutenant Bill Reid, was hit in the head and shoulders by shell splinters, and his face was full of Perspex fragments. Pulling his goggles down to protect his eyes from the icy blast, Reid got the stricken Lancaster under control after a loss of 2,000 feet. At first bothered by blood running into his eyes, he soon found that the freezing air coagulated the flow. Reid said nothing about his injuries and pressed on.

Within minutes the Lancaster was struck again, this time by a Focke-Wulf 190, which raked the whole length of the bomber's fuselage with its fire. The navigator was killed, the wireless operator mortally wounded, and both the flight engineer and Reid were hit. Cannon shells disrupted the oxygen system and further damaged the turrets and hydraulics.

After the loss of another 2,000 feet, Reid leveled out and, arms wrapped round the control column to hold the nose up and full left rudder to keep straight, maintained the course for Dusseldorf. "It was only common sense to keep going," he said. "Turning back against the bomber stream would have been dangerous." Steering by occasional reference to the Pole Star, Dusseldorf was reached and the bombs delivered on target.

On the way home, the crew survived passage through a heavy flak barrage, the temporary failure of all four engines when a fuel tank emptied unexpectedly, and the drag of bomb doors that could not be closed. However, the strain of holding the aircraft straight and level began to tell on the pilot. Reid lost more blood as his wounds reopened and he went through periods of exhaustion and light-headedness. At last he crossed the English coast and managed to recover sufficiently to land at Shipdam, a USAF base, only to have a much damaged undercarriage collapse on touchdown. On recovery from his injuries, Bill Reid found, much to his expressed astonishment, that he had been awarded the Victoria Cross.

Left: In 1995 Dan Patterson photographed Bill Reid at the controls of *Just Jane,* on the tarmac at the Lincolnshire Aviation Heritage Museum, a former Bomber Command airfield at East Kirkby, Lincolnshire.

P-51 Mustang

Scourge of the Luftwaffe

Shortly after World War II began in 1939, the British government established a purchasing commission in the United States. One of its tasks was to order U.S. fighter aircraft for the RAF. At the time, the choice was very limited. Of the U.S. aircraft available, only the Curtiss P-40 came close to matching the levels of performance needed, but the Curtiss plant was running at capacity, so even that fighter was in short supply. North American Aviation was asked if the P-40 could be manufactured under licence from Curtiss. The response was that North American could produce a better aircraft and get it in the air more quickly. The prototype first flew on October 26, 1940, just 178 days after the order had been placed. In general, the aircraft handled well and the design allowed for a massive fuel load. However, it was soon clear that its performance, although good below 15,000 feet, could not match Luftwaffe fighters at higher altitudes. The first Mustang Is, powered by Allison engines, were delivered to the RAF in October 1941 and made their combat debut over France on May 5, 1942. With their long range and excellent low-level performance, they were well suited to tactical reconnaissance and ground-attack missions.

In April 1942, Ronnie Harker from Rolls-Royce's Flight Test establishment flew the Mustang and was impressed with the way the fighter handled. He thought that re-engining the Mustang with a Merlin 61 would solve the altitude problem. The result of the conversion was astonishing. The combination of North American's superb aerodynamics and a Rolls-Royce engine produced an aircraft that could, with drop tanks, fly to Berlin and match the Luftwaffe's fighters at altitude when it got

A P-51B painted in the distinctive black and white stripes of the D-Day invasion, this fighter of the 357th Fighter Group, *Kalamazoo Kid,* flown by Lieutenant Charles S. Pearson, was lost on February 10, 1945. **Opposite:** The yellow tips of the 11-foot propeller etch a circle as the Merlin engine warms up. Butch Schroeder's award-winning restored Mustang is marked in the colors of Clyde East, who flew for the 15th Tactical Reconnaissance Squadron, 10th Photographic Group. *Lil' Margaret* is an F-6D, the photographic reconnaissance version of the P-51D.

there. American production of the Mustang with the Merlin engine began in early 1943, and P-51Bs and Cs started arriving in England in August and October 1943.

The P-51D, which appeared over Europe in the spring of 1944, was the definitive version of the Mustang. One of the problems had been poor pilot visibility to the rear. The British field-modified some Mustangs with fishbowl-shaped canopies called Malcolm Hoods, which helped, but North American decided that visibility could be improved still further. P-51Ds were fitted with bubble canopies based on those used by the Hawker Typhoon. The new design offered pilots unrestricted vision in all directions with virtually no distortion.

Prewar U.S. air power doctrine held that large formations of heavy bombers flying in daylight at high altitudes would be able to defend themselves against enemy interceptors. By the summer of 1943, the Eighth Air Force was committed to deep penetration raids over Germany beyond the range of available escort fighters. German fighter reaction to these raids was fierce and bomber losses were so severe that the future of daylight bombing hung in the balance. The Lockheed P-38 Lightning had the range to escort the bombers, but few were available in the United Kingdom and it was difficult to maintain. The Republic P-47 Thunderbolt was more suitable as an escort but did not then have sufficient range.

The solution to the long-range fighter problem was largely unrecognized at first. Eager though the Eighth Air Force was to get hold of Mustangs, the first P-51 went to General Brereton's Ninth Air Force, with its principal role that of supporting the

Once it was mated with the Rolls-Royce Merlin engine, the Mustang became one of the greatest fighters ever.
When fitted with the drop tanks seen here, it had the range to escort the American bombers all the way to their targets deep into Germany.
Butch Schroeder, seen here flying his restored fighter, has installed the teardrop tanks.

Allied armies in the invasion of Europe. General William Kepner, commander of VIII Fighter Command, deplored the arbitrary assignment of P-51s as tactical aircraft, insisting that "developments in Germany [made the P-51] the only satisfactory answer." The P-51 got its chance when agreement was reached in October 1943 for all fighter units in the U.K. to support bombers engaged in Operation Pointblank (the Allied combined bomber offensive agreed upon at the Casablanca Conference in January 1943) until further notice.

The first Merlin-engined P-51B Mustangs to arrive in England went to the 354th Fighter Group, and began operations on December 1, 1943, under the temporary leadership of Lieutenant Colonel Don Blakeslee. He had flown 120 fighter sweeps with the RAF before transferring to the USAAF to become deputy Commanding Officer of the 4th Fighter Group, the unit he would command after seeing the 354th through their P-51 conversion. The 354th was soon in the thick of things, shooting down 16 enemy fighters without loss during a mission to Kiel on January 5, 1944. On January 11, they repeated the performance, with Major Jim Howard being awarded the Medal of Honor for his protection of a B-17 wing in an hour-long solo battle with some 30 Luftwaffe

fighters. He was credited with three confirmed kills and a number of others damaged. His Mustang had a single bullet hole in the left wing.

In early 1944 the character of the air battle over Europe changed dramatically as P-51s became more plentiful. To the Germans, the appearance of USAAF fighters over the Reich was disturbing, and the Mustang came as a considerable shock. Here was a fighter that could reach Berlin, and was superior to the Bf 109 and Fw 190 in terms of speed and turning ability. If the German aircraft had better rates of climb, they could not outdive the P-51 and could not match its zoom climb. The Fw 190's only noticeable advantage was in rate of roll, and even that diminished at high speeds. To quote Major Robert Riemensnider, commander of the 55th Fighter Squadron: "The P-51 had speed, range, and an all-round versatility that was unsurpassed by any of its contemporaries in combat service." P-51 groups claimed some 4,950 aircraft shot down (approximately 50 percent of all USAAF claims in the European theatre) and 4,131 destroyed on the ground. Losses were some 840 Mustangs. Top-scoring P-51 unit was the Ninth Air Force's 354th Fighter Group, with 701 air claims and 255 ground claims.

Right: Don Gentile of the 4th Fighter Group, seen here after returning to the U.S. for a promotional tour. Gentile was credited with 21-plus aerial victories. General Dwight D. Eisenhower called Gentile a "one-man air force" upon presenting him with the Distinguished Flying Cross in April 1942. **Below:** A collection of the flight gear and personal items issued to Mustang pilots and their ground crews. From the right: A pilot's leather A-2 flight jacket, an aerial chart, the USAAF Pilot's Information Manual. Center: Many American pilots preferred the RAF leather flying helmets and RAF goggles; the North American Aviation Flight Manual for the P-51. Left: A ground crewman's sheepskin lined jacket, over a mechanic's HBT coveralls. Bottom left: Most essential, paper for writing letters home.

D.H. Mosquito

Wooden Wonder

WHEN DE HAVILLAND PROPOSED building a wooden aircraft to take advantage of the underused resources of the furniture industry at a time of great pressure on the aircraft industry, and when steel and aluminium were in short supply, the Air Ministry showed little interest. In 1938, de Havilland began the design of the Mosquito as a private venture. Only when the first prototype flew in November 1940 and gave evidence of having a startling performance did the Ministry show any real enthusiasm for the project. So confident were de Havilland that the Mosquito would prove to be at least as fast as any other aircraft that the design included no defensive armament.

Originally conceived as a fast day bomber, the Mosquito had such speed, agility and exceptional durability that it was adapted for a variety of roles. It became a tactical bomber, pathfinder, day or night fighter, fighter-bomber, intruder, maritime strike and photo-reconnaissance aircraft. As one pilot described flying it: "The Mosquito was a fairly heavy airplane…but it was very light on the controls once you got it in the air. It was maneuverable as hell, but it wouldn't turn with a single-engine fighter. Of course, we could outrun a 109 or 190, as long as it didn't have an altitude advantage." It was primarily flown by the RAF, RAAF, RCAF, RNZAF and USAAF, but also saw service with a number of other air forces at various times, including those of Belgium, Burma, China, Czechoslovakia, France, Israel, Norway, South Africa, the Soviet Union, Sweden, Turkey, Yugoslavia and the Dominican Republic. Between 1940 and 1950, there were 7,781 Mosquitos built.

The Mosquito's capacity to penetrate defences and to strike targets accurately made it ideal for use as a pathfinder, marking targets with flares for attack by massive formations of the less precise heavy bomber force. Mosquitos flown by the RAF's Light Night Striking Force targeted small but vital installations, where precision was of great importance, and they acted as a diversion force, simulating large formations through the use of chaff, so drawing attention to themselves and away from the heavy bombers. If no heavy bomber raids were planned on a particular night, the LNSF would often carry out smaller scale raids to ensure that the German defences got no rest.

For Operation Jericho, carried out on February 18, 1944, nineteen Mosquitos set out to destroy the walls of Amiens prison to allow the escape of some 700 members of the French resistance, many of whom who were awaiting execution. The bombs were released from very low altitude and accurately placed. Over 250 of the prisoners escaped through holes blown in the prison walls. In a similar raid on April 11, 1944, six Mosquitos of 613 Squadron flew to The Hague in Holland. Their target was the Gestapo-controlled Dutch Central Population Registry in the Kliez-kamp Art Galleries, which the Dutch Resistance had requested destroyed. Flying at 50 feet, the Mosquitos placed two bombs through the front doors of the building and another two through the windows on each side. The target was totally destroyed and only one aircraft was slightly damaged. Pilot Officer Clarence Murl Jasper, an American in the Royal Canadian Air Force, born in Ottawa, Kansas, said about low-flying in the Mosquito: "These missions were difficult for the navigators because they were trying to determine our position from an altitude of below 20 feet. We would cross rivers and railroad tracks and, of course, never fly along them, or we'd run into a flak

A photo-reconnaissance de Havilland Mosquito operated by the USAAF. **Opposite:** This Mosquito was flown to the National Museum of the USAF in Dayton, Ohio, in the 1980s. The very fast twin-engine aircraft was used in many roles during World War II. Seen here in the hangar at Wright Field, where aircraft are prepared for exhibit, the same aircraft appears on the following page, transformed from a bomber version in RAF markings into the USAAF aerial reconnaissance version.

John Cunningham was a legendary test pilot for de Havilland after World War II. In 1941, he became the RAF's first night-fighter ace while flying the Bristol Beaufighter. In 1940 he test-flew the prototype Mosquito, seen here. The yellow-painted fighter is exhibited at the small de Havilland Museum near Hatfield, north of London.

tower sooner or later. When we crossed a river or a track at such low altitudes, we were never sure of where we were. And flying so low, we nearly always flew under power lines and bridges."

Between 1943 and the end of the war, Mosquitos were also used as transport aircraft between Leuchars in Scotland and Stockholm. Lockheed Hudsons and Lodestars were also used, but these slower aircraft could only fly this route at night or in bad weather to avoid the risk of being shot down. During the long daylight hours of summer, the Mosquito was the only safe alternative. Sweden was neutral, so the aircraft had civilian markings and were flown by Norwegian officers, who were nominally civilian aircrew of BOAC. They carried high-value cargos such as precision ball bearings, and important passengers were occasionally accommodated in an improvised cabin in the bomb bay.

In service with Bomber Command, Mosquitos flew over 28,000 operations and dropped 35,000 tons of bombs. In the process, 193 Mosquitos were lost. This was a loss rate of 0.7 percent, compared to a 2.2-percent loss rate for the four-engined heavy bombers. It has been calculated that a Mosquito could have been armed with a 4,000-pound bomb, flown to Germany and dropped the bomb, returned to base and repeated the operation, and still have landed before a Stirling (the slowest of the heavy bombers) launched at the same time carrying two 4,000-pound bombs. It is no surprise to find that a Mosquito holds the record for the most missions flown by an Allied bomber in WWII. *F for Freddie* (serial LR 503) was a Mk. IX that flew 213 operational sorties during the war, only to crash at Calgary on May 10, 1945, two days after VE Day.

This is the same Mosquito as on the previous page, now appearing as a USAAF PR XVI used for reconnaissance by the 25th Bomb Group, Eight Air Force. Based at RAF Watton, these fast aircraft flew weather missions, and arrived over the target for the day about 20 minutes before the bomber forces, reporting on weather, clouds and enemy fighter activity. After the strike, the Mosquito would return and provide photographic results of the raid.

Messerschmitt Me 262

Swallow and Stormbird

ALTHOUGH THE MESSERSCHMITT ME 262 Schwalbe (Swallow, known to the Allies as Stormbird) did not appear in combat until the later stages of World War II, it originated as an experimental project in 1939. Its development and introduction to service were delayed by a combination of bureaucratic indifference, shortage of funds, the technical problems of a revolutionary design, and Hitler's procrastination. Among the host of teething troubles experienced were the poor reliability of the Junkers Jumo axial-flow jet engines, which had a life of only 25 hours at best, and inferior tires that frequently burst under the stress of 120-mph touchdowns. Nevertheless, when it did make an appearance, it was clear that, whatever faults it had, when it was serviceable, the Me 262's performance was superior to that of any Allied aircraft available at the time.

The twin-engined swept-wing Swallow was capable of 540 miles per hour and could climb to 30,000 feet in seven minutes. Complementing this impressive performance was the Me 262's heavy armament of four closely grouped 30 mm cannon, which could destroy a heavy bomber in one short burst. At a time when the air war seemed all but over, it faced Allied airmen, particularly those involved in the daylight bomber offensive, with a daunting threat. However, because of its developmental problems and Hitler's insistence that it should be brought into service initially as a fast bomber for use against the Allied invasion force, the first unit of Me 262 interceptors was not declared operational until October 1944, and even then they were rarely seen by Allied aircrew. Me 262s flew more than 50 sorties in a day only once, on April 7, 1945. On

A wartime image of an Me 262 caught on film by a P-51 Mustang. The gun camera runs when the guns are firing. **Opposite:** A nose-on view displays the shark-like shape and streamlined design of this Me 262 1a, the first operational combat jet fighter, now at the National Museum of the USAF. The ominous gun ports reveal the four 30 mm cannons it carries. Concentrated cannon fire from this fast German fighter could destroy a four-engine bomber in short order.

that day the Eighth Air Force alone flew 1,261 bombers and 830 fighters over Germany.

General Adolf Galland described the Me 262 as a docile, pilot's aircraft. He said of his first flight, "It flew as if there was an angel pushing." According to Lieutenant Jorg Czypionka, the Me 262 was not as hard to fly as reported. "They told us to handle it carefully, and as long as you did things right, it would not turn and bite you; but we were young and wouldn't have cared even if it was more dangerous. The main thing was that if you could fly it at all and get the enemy in your sights, you had them. The gun armament was fantastic. One burst was all it took." Nevertheless, flying training presented the Luftwaffe with unexpected difficulties. Preparing even experienced pilots to cope with a temperamental first-generation jet aircraft often proved anything but simple, and it took longer than predicted for units to become operational. Then there were the relentless attentions of the Allied air forces. Me 262s and their spares had to struggle through a German transport system devastated by bombing, and, knowing that the jets were most vulnerable during takeoff and landing, USAAF fighter pilots began to haunt jet airfields. On October 7, 1944, Lieutenant Urban Drew flying a P-51 of the 361st Fighter Group caught two Me 262s just after they had taken off and shot both of them down before they could accelerate away. Once up to speed, the Me 262 was a difficult opponent, and an experienced Luftwaffe pilot had the choice of initiating or refusing combat as he wished. Even then, the best of them sometimes got caught by the persistent Mustangs. Walter Nowotny, a Luftwaffe ace with

ACHTUNG!
Am BUGRAD
NICHT SCHLEPPEN

Walter Schuck, seen here in the cockpit of the National Air and Space Museum Messerschmitt Bf 109, was a leading Luftwaffe ace with 206 aerial victories, eight of them while flying the Messerschmitt Me 262.

258 aerial victories, was killed on November 8, 1944, after attacking a B-17 formation and running the gauntlet of its P-51 escort. On April 26, 1945, the celebrated fighter leader Adolf Galland was caught by a burst of fire from a P-47. He was wounded in the knee and forced to land his badly damaged Me 262 on an airfield being strafed by U.S. fighters. Even Galland, one of the world's most capable fighter pilots, flying the most advanced fighter aircraft in the world, could not escape the USAAF's implacable pursuit.

Galland, a veteran of the Battle of Britain who claimed 104 victories by the end of the war, had disagreed violently with both Hitler and Göring over the decision to deploy the Me 262 as a bomber. In January 1945 matters came to a head when Göring met his fighter leaders to hear their grievances. This became known as the Fighters Revolt, and Galland was subsequently dismissed from his position as General of Fighters. He asked permission to return to active combat duty and was allowed to

form his own unit, Jagdverband 44, equipped with Me 262s. He began gathering together as many of Germany's aces as he could, creating a unique unit with a glittering array of talented pilots, including Barkhorn (301 victories), Bär (220), Steinhoff (176), Lützow (108) and Krupinski (197). On March 31, 1945, Galland led his new formation to Munich-Riem, where JV 44 established its headquarters and commenced operations against the USAAF's daylight raids pulverizing Germany at the time. During its one month of operations, JV 44 was credited with the destruction of 45 enemy aircraft before being overrun by Allied forces at Salzburg on May 3, 1945.

Slightly over 1,400 Me 262s of all its versions were produced. Due to fuel shortages, pilot shortages, and the lack of many airfields that could support the Me 262 (concrete runways were needed since the jet engines melted tar), only some 200 Me 262s made it to combat units.

In many ways a precursor to modern cockpits, the cockpit of the Me 262 has a simple layout with flight instruments on the left and engine display on the right. Although the stick had controls not found on the American aircraft of the time, at this early stage of jet fighter development the cockpit was not pressurized.

F-86 Sabre

The Elegant Blade

THE NORTH AMERICAN F-86 SABRE was an elegant second-generation jet fighter. It was the essential counter to the MiGs during the war in Korea, and an important element of NATO air forces in the early years of the Cold War. From a pilot's point of view, it was a delight to fly, with well-harmonized controls and a forgiving nature. The Sabre combined what American aircraft designers had discovered through their own work on early jet aircraft with German research data captured after World War II. The result was an outstanding basic design, capable of considerable further development and easily adaptable to roles other than that of the classic day interceptor.

The first XP-86 prototype was rolled out on August 8, 1947, and made its first flight on October 1. The pilot was George "Wheaties" Welch, North American's chief test pilot. The first flight in the XP-86 was uneventful, until it came time to land and Welch found that the nosewheel leg wouldn't lock down. Welch made a firm nose-up landing, and the nosewheel snapped into place after the main wheels hit the runway. Welch muttered over the radio: "Lucky! Lucky!" Welch was at Pearl Harbor when the Japanese attacked on December 7, 1941, and was one of the few USAAF pilots to get a Curtiss P-40 into the air to fight back. He remained in the Pacific theater and scored 16 aerial victories before joining North American as a test pilot in 1944. He was with the company until 1954, when he was killed ejecting from an F-100 Super Sabre during high-speed testing.

It is recorded that Welch flew the XP-86 through the sound barrier in a shallow dive on October 19, 1947, making it the first aircraft intended for series production to fly faster than sound.

Colonel James K. Johnson was wing commander of the famed 4th Fighter Interceptor Wing, flying F-86 Sabres. The "Mayor of Sabre Jet City" entered the record books on March 28, 1953, when he became the 29th jet ace. **Opposite:** The F-86 Sabre, an elegant swept-wing jet, was a fighter pilot's fighter, a delight to fly and capable of becoming supersonic in a dive. This Sabre is at the National Museum of the USAF.

However, there is evidence to suggest that, without telling the North American management, he had gone beyond the parameters of his flight test program and exceeded Mach 1 several times before the first officially recognized supersonic flight of the Bell X-1 on October 14. Lacking adequate instrumentation in the cockpit at the time, Welch could not prove that he had been supersonic, but his earlier flight profiles were similar to that flown on October 19 and what appeared to be sonic booms were heard by people on the ground several times on October 1 and afterward.

The USAF began testing the XP-86 in early December 1947. Major Ken Chilstrom, the USAF test pilot, concluded that "the Air Force now had the very best jet fighter developed to this date, anywhere in the world." The first P-86A flew on May 20, 1948, and on September 15 the USAF publicly demonstrated the capabilities of their new fighter when an F-86A set a world air speed record of 671 miles per hour. With the flight test program complete and the fighter suitably launched on the world stage, the USAF took delivery of the first two operational F-86As on February 15, 1949. (The USAF replaced the P for Pursuit designation with F for Fighter on June 10, 1948.)

The first real test of the F-86's combat capabilities came during the Korean War. When United Nations forces approached the Yalu River in November 1950, the Chinese intervened with a massive ground offensive accompanied by an unexpectedly potent threat in the air — the MiG-15, a swept-wing Soviet fighter. It was quickly apparent that none of the UN aircraft operating in Korea were a match for the MiG-15. It was some 100 miles per hour faster than the USAF's F-80C, could climb to 50,000 feet, and was heavily armed with one 37 mm and

Walker "Bud" Mahurin, WWII and Korean War ace, thought the F-86 cockpit was "fine, but the exciting thing was it had a swept wing and it could go like hell…. The controls and instruments were close to hand and easy to reach. The landing gear lever had a wheel on it so you couldn't grab something else and think you were lowering or raising the landing gear."

two 23 mm cannon. On December 10, 1950, the escort carrier *Cape Esperance* arrived in Tokyo Bay with a load of F-86As of the USAF 4th Fighter Wing. Four of these went into combat from an advanced Korean airfield on December 17. On that mission, Lieutenant Colonel Bruce Hinton shot down the first MiG-15 to fall victim to the Sabre.

The F-86 was not quite as good in the climb nor at very high altitude as the lighter MiG-15, nor did its six 0.5-inch machine guns have the hitting power of its opponent's cannon, but it was just as fast and was more stable as a gun platform at high Mach numbers. It also had the advantage of being fitted with a radar-ranging gunsight. Equally important, the Sabre was a joy to fly, whereas the MiG-15 had a tendency to flick savagely if driven too hard in high-G turns. With balancing features on each side, the decisive factor proved to be the high standard of training enjoyed by the USAF pilots. Although it was never possible for the UN forces to establish and maintain air supremacy all over North

Korea, the consistent superiority of the F-86 in combat was never in doubt. By the end of the war, the USAF claimed to have shot down 792 MiGs for a loss of only 76 Sabres, and 11 USAF pilots were credited with 10 aerial victories or more. Captain Joseph McConnell headed the list with 16. "Bud'" Mahurin, already an ace with 20.5 victories in WWII, added 3.5 to his total in Korea. He described the F-86 as "a brilliant design. The F-86 was a Cadillac, the MiG-15 was a Model T Ford. You had a sense of power, a sense of high performance. You didn't think much about the airplane. It felt like a part of you. In combat, you didn't think I'm going to turn now, and I'm going to pull back on the stick. You just did it automatically, like moving an extension of your body."

F-86s saw service with 36 nations and were used in combat by Pakistan, Argentina, Portugal, South Africa, Taiwan and Venezuela. They were manufactured in the United States, Canada, Australia, Japan and Italy, with a total production of all variants of 9,860.

This F-86H, also displayed at the National Museum of the USAF, shows the fighter without its skin, revealing how densely packed the aircraft of the 20th century were becoming. Compare this to the Bleriot from the earliest days of aviation on pages 10 and 11. Most visible are the yellow oxygen tanks for high-altitude flying and the 20 mm cannons.

MiG-15

Soviet Surprise

TURBO-JET DEVELOPMENT IN THE Soviet Union did not really begin until after World War II, when the fruits of German and British technology became available. In the preface to the 1948 edition of *Jane's All the World's Aircraft,* the editor wrote: "Since the war, Russia has made good use of the Eastern German industry. Experimental establishments, factories, equipment, prototypes, and, in particular, technicians have all been taken over and this accession of technical equipment, knowledge and personnel, merged into Russia's gigantic aircraft industry and industrial potential, has no doubt been responsible for the remarkable progress which has taken place in recent years."

Soviet efforts were given a boost when, in 1946, the British government agreed to the export of Rolls-Royce Nene centrifugal-flow engines to the Soviet Union. By 1948 the MiG-15 was in production, a swept-wing design built around the Nene and promising a performance to surpass anything being flown in the West.

The MiG-15 (NATO codename Fagot) was conceived as a counter to U.S. bombers such as the B-29 and so featured heavy cannon armament — two 23 mm cannon and a single 37 mm cannon. These destructive weapons gave the MiG-15 a punch powerful enough to destroy a bomber with just a few rounds, but their slow rate of fire made it more difficult to achieve hits on small, fast jet fighters. The 23 mm and 37 mm weapons also differed in their ballistics, and some United Nations pilots during the Korean War had the unnerving experience of having 23 mm shells fly over them while the 37 mm shells passed by beneath.

On November 8, 1950, the world's first all-jet combat took place over Korea when F-80Cs of the 51st Fighter Interceptor Wing were jumped by MiG-15s. In a brief exchange, the USAF scored first blood, Lieutenant Russell Brown shooting down one of the attackers. However, F-80Cs were no match for MiG-15s, and even when the first F-86s entered combat in December, it was clear to the pilots of the USAF's new fighter that the MiG-15 had to be treated with respect. USAF bomber crews had already learned that lesson. B-29s had pounded industrial and transportation targets north of Seoul, and cratered the runways of airfields the Chinese were preparing in North Korea, preventing the basing of MiGs south of the Yalu. Important as this B-29 achievement was, it had a cost. On October 23, 1951, for example, eight B-29s and their escorts were attacked by MiG-15s. Three of the bombers were shot down and the rest so severely damaged that they never flew again. Soon afterward, the B-29s were restricted to night operations. Constraints of this kind brought the USAF to the realization that the MiG-15 had put air supremacy over North Korea beyond the reach of UN forces.

In mid-1951, MiG-15s fitted with drop tanks expanded their area of operations. "Trains" of MiGs 60 to 80 strong flew down the center of the Korean peninsula at high altitude, elements peeling off at intervals to challenge the patrolling F-86s. The main body continued south, converging over P'yongyang with a similar formation coming from the east coast. The resulting force of 100 or so then dropped down to search for UN fighter-bombers on interdiction sorties. The fighter-bombers often had to jettison their weapons under, and by September 1951, they were restricted to areas south of the Ch'ongch'on River.

Colonel Yevgeni Georgievich Pepelyayev *(right)* was one of best MiG-15 pilots and was among the top aces of the war. He commanded the 196th IAP, 324th IAD. **Opposite:** On September 21, 1953, Lieutenant Kim Sok No defected and flew his MiG-15bis to Kimpo Air Base in South Korea. He seemed genuinely unaware that a reward of $100,000 had been offered to anyone who defected to the West with a MiG-15. The aircraft on display at the National Museum of the USAF is that same MiG-15.

This was the period that the "Honchos" (a nickname given to experienced Soviet MiG pilots) were in Korea. Their most successful month was October 1951, when eight MiGs flown by Soviet pilots were lost, but they claimed eight F-86s, six F-84Es, two RF-80A, one F-80C, one Meteor and ten B-29s. During that period over 30 Soviet MiG-15 pilots were recognized as aces, among them Nikolai Sutyagin (13 kills); Yevgeni Pepelyayev (12), Lev Shchukin (10), Sergei Kramarenko (7), Mikhail Ponomaryev (5), and Dmitri Samoylov (5). (These figures, confirmed by the UN, are lower than the original Soviet claims.) Shchukin's most significant victory came on October 2, 1951. During an intense dogfight with F-86s, he saw a fellow pilot bail out, but then caught the victorious U.S. pilot by surprise, closed to short range and hit the F-86 with a solid burst. Badly shot-up, the F-86 disengaged, trailing black smoke. It was later confirmed that Shchukin had severely damaged the F-86E *Lady Frances* flown by Colonel Francis Gabreski of the 4th Fighter Interceptor Wing. However,

on January 11, 1952, in an incredible twist of fate, Gabreski and Shchukin met for a second time, and this time Gabreski forced the Soviet pilot to eject.

Toward the end of 1951, a different pattern of MiG-15 activity was noticed. Large groups of MiGs maneuvered south of the Yalu, staying at maximum altitude and keeping well clear of F-86s. Over a six-week period, the formations became steadily bolder. Then the cycle started again. It appeared that courses were being run by the Soviets to provide an introduction to combat for new pilots. The innovations made little difference to the way aerial battles went in 1952, when MiGs were claimed at an average rate of one per day, while F-86 losses averaged one per week. The introduction of the F-86F with a redesigned wing and more powerful engine left the MiG-15 without any real advantages.

The USSR built around 12,000 MiG-15s in all variants and it was widely exported. It was also built under license in Czechoslovakia (as the S-102 and S-103) and Poland (Lim-1 and Lim-2).

A restored ex Polish Air Force MiG-15 UTI Fagot/Midget over the western United States. The two-seat version of the famous Russian designed aircraft was used for training flights. This image made by Warsaw based air-to-air photographer Mariusz Adamski.

The cockpit of Lieutenant No's MiG-15. He said that the main problem was the lack of power-boosted controls, which made the MiG very heavy to fly. Note the Chinese characters written in red paint on the instrument panel. In 1950, UN forces in Korea were taken by surprise by the combat capability of the MiG-15, which was quickly seen to be superior in almost every respect to the F-80s and Meteors of the Allies.

Lockheed Constellation

"Connie"

THE LOCKHEED CONSTELLATION WAS conceived in 1939 by Howard Hughes and designed by Kelly Johnson. The result was one of the most distinctive aircraft ever built. While the DC-4 had an essentially practical, no-nonsense appearance, the Constellation was a beauty of subtly blending curves. Its nose drooped to shorten the nose-wheel leg, and the dolphin-like fuselage tapered gracefully toward the rear, sweeping upwards to carry the triple-finned tail. Beneath its attractive exterior the "Connie" held many innovative features, including powered flying controls and the first reversible-pitch propellers used to shorten the landing run of a civil airliner. It was pressurized to allow operations above 20,000 feet and its four 2200-horsepower supercharged engines gave it a cruising speed of 280 miles per hour, thus stealing a considerable march on the competition. The first prototype did not fly until January 9, 1943, with Eddie Allen as captain, on loan from Boeing, and Lockheed's Milo Burcham as copilot. They completed a ferry hop from Burbank to Muroc Field, California, from where the L-049 would continue its test flying. The test program did not always go smoothly. The troublesome Wright R-3350 Cyclone engine was being used (the engine used in the Boeing B-29) and the Connie was bedeviled by some familiar problems, all too frequently suffering from overheating and engine fires. Another more successful feature founded on previous experience was the Lockheed wing, which was effectively the same as that of the P-38 Lightning, differing only in scale. The distinctive triple-fin design was adopted to ensure that the aircraft's overall height was kept low enough so that it would fit into existing hangars.

Kelly Johnson's beautifully crafted airliner, seen here in Western Airlines markings. Western Airlines was absorbed by Delta in the late 1980s. **Opposite:** The full majesty of a Constellation. Often described as the most beautiful and elegant airliner ever built, the Constellation first flew in 1943 and continued to evolve until 1958; by that time, 856 had been built.

It was intended to give Hughes' TWA a marked advantage over the DC-4s of American and United, and in 1943 the early flights of the first Constellation confirmed its promise. However, the demands of the war being paramount, the early production models followed the DC-4 into military service as C-69s. With a flash of showmanship, Hughes and TWA president Jack Frye delivered the prototype to the USAAF, painting it in TWA red and flying it from Burbank to Washington in under six hours and 58 minutes, half an hour less than Hughes' own transcontinental record set in 1937. During another flight, the aircraft stopped at Wright Field, Dayton, and took Orville Wright into the air for the last time, more than 40 years after his historic first flight. He commented that the wingspan on the Constellation was longer than the distance of his first flight.

TWA finally took delivery of ten Model L-049 Constellations toward the end of 1945 and on February 15, 1946, advertised the opening of its transcontinental service with another theatrical flourish from Hughes. Gathering a bevy of Hollywood's famous together, including such luminaries as Paulette Goddard, Veronica Lake, Virginia Mayo, Linda Darnell, William Powell, Walter Pidgeon and Edward G. Robinson, he flew them from Los Angeles to New York. That month also saw Pan American flying Constellations to Bermuda and TWA taking them across the Atlantic to Paris. On June 17, 1947, Pan American World Airways opened the first ever regularly scheduled around-the-world service with their L749 Clipper *America*.

A rash of incidents in 1945 and 1946 grounded the Connie for six weeks. It was found the aircraft had no basic flaws and it was again pronounced airworthy, though engine problems continued,

In addition to its role as transport aircraft, the Constellation also had a long career as a military aircraft. The "Connie" was also adapted to the role of airborne radar. The EC-121 Warning Star used in the Vietnam War provided early warning detection of MiGs approaching U.S. aircraft.

giving rise to a "Best Tri-Motor" label. One Connie actually did fly as a trimotor. On June 18, 1946, Pan Am's NC88858 had an engine fire while climbing out over the Atlantic. The fire in Number 4 engine burned through the engine mount, causing the entire engine assembly to drop into the Atlantic. The aircraft diverted to a small emergency field and was landed without further mishap. Pan Am mechanics determined the aircraft needed factory repair, which meant moving the Connie to Burbank, California. They removed the ragged pieces of the engine nacelle, faired over the hole in the wing with sheets of aluminum, and flew the Connie 2,450 miles to the Lockheed factory with three engines.

Lockheed continued to improve the breed until, in 1951, the Super Constellation appeared. With its fuselage lengthened, the Super Connie's graceful lines were even more elegant. Powered by Wright R-3350 Turbo-Compound double-row radials of 3,250 horsepower and fitted with tip tanks, the Model L1049G could cruise at 330 miles per hour and had a maximum range of 4,800 miles. It could accommodate up to 100 passengers and its all-up weight reached 140,000 pounds, compared to the 86,000 pounds of the L049. One more variant, the L1649 Starliner, flew in 1956. It had a longer wing and an increased range. On September 29, 1957, a Starliner flew from Los Angeles to London in 18 hours and 32 minutes. The L-1649A still holds the record for the longest-duration nonstop passenger flight. During TWA's inaugural London to San Francisco flight on 1/2 October 1957, the aircraft stayed aloft for 23 hours and 19 minutes.

The Starliner was the last of a distinguished line and had a claim to being the ultimate expression of the piston-powered airliner. The last scheduled passenger flight of a piston-engined airliner in the United States was made by a TWA L-749 on May 11, 1967, but Constellations continued to serve as fast freighters for years afterward. Lockheed built 856 Constellations (331 of these for the military). More than one Connie has been anchored to the ground and used as a restaurant or cocktail lounge. General Dwight Eisenhower used a C-121A military named *Columbine* as his personal aircraft, and another, named *Columbine II,* after he became President.

This EC-121, nicknamed "Triple Nickel" because of its serial number (53-555) and now at the National Museum of the USAF, saw action in the Vietnam war. On October 24, 1967, over the Gulf of Tonkin, it guided a U.S. fighter by radar into position to destroy a MiG-21. It was the first time a weapons controller aboard an airborne radar aircraft had ever directed a successful attack on an enemy plane.

DHC Beaver

Creature of the Bush

IN NOVEMBER 1946, A DE HAVILLAND CANADA questionnaire asked eighty experienced Canadian pilots to describe the ideal bush aircraft. The responses led to the DHC-2 Beaver, the prototype of which flew on August 16, 1947, piloted by Russ Bannock, the company's chief test pilot and Canada's top-scoring night fighter ace. The Beaver was designed specifically to meet the challenges of remote, undeveloped regions, and it came to be regarded with great affection by the people it served. It can carry a crew of two, plus six passengers or more than 1,500 pounds of cargo at a maximum speed of 180 miles per hour as a landplane or 155 miles per hour as a floatplane, and its maximum range is 800 miles. Like the Russian An-2, the Beaver is a tough, relatively simple aircraft powered by a single radial engine and equipped with high-lift devices to allow it to operate from small, unsophisticated airstrips. Its oil reservoir filling spout is located inside the cockpit and the oil can be refilled while the aircraft is in flight. It converts rapidly from carrying freight to seating seven passengers, and can be fitted with a conventional tailwheel undercarriage, skis, floats, or amphibious pontoons. It is the quintessential bush pilot's aircraft, and has been a common sight on the lakes, rivers and icefields of the northernmost reaches of the North American continent for over half a century. The Beaver has become a symbol of the far north, and has found use as a bush plane all over the world. An Ontario Lands and Forests Beaver aircraft made the first recorded fire-bombing attack in Canada in the 1950s, dropping water-filled paper bags on a fire north of Sault Ste. Marie, Ontario.

The design of the Beaver took account of the fact that it was to be a flying pickup truck, and would have to withstand the challenge

A USAF Beaver in a typical Alaska setting, shown unloading for a group of waiting huskies to take over. **Opposite:** The de Havilland Canada Beaver on floats exhibited at the Canada Aviation Museum in Ottawa is CF-FHB, the prototype Beaver. It flew for the first time on August 16, 1947.

of rough treatment, so strength was a priority. Many of the remote settlements that the aircraft would have to visit had no conventional airfields available and even when airstrips were available, they were often rudimentary and spent a good amount of the year covered in snow. This meant that the Beaver had to be a true STOL (short takeoff and landing) aircraft. It features a high-lift wing with its entire trailing edge hinged, hydraulically operated flaps and slotted ailerons. These allow the aircraft to take off and land in extremely short distances. As Russell Bannock, the Beaver's first test pilot and later head of de Havilland Canada, says "It's designed as a STOL aircraft to get in and out of small lakes and short strips… it's a marvelous aircraft to fly." He remembers a trial flown against a Cessna 195 floatplane, and says: "When the Cessna first broke the water, I was at 300 feet in the Beaver." The ability to haul huge loads and to get off the water in 560 feet and land in 500 is why lodge operators and backcountry fishing and hunting outfitters love Beavers. Company test pilots testify that on wheels in zero wind with full load they can get airborne in just 650 feet. Under similar wind and load conditions, the floatplane version will unstick to clear a 50-foot obstacle in 1,165 feet. Beavers are certified to fly with a canoe strapped to the floats and they have carried such varied loads as lumber, snowmobiles, hot tubs, sheets of plywood, trail bikes, and propane cylinders. The bush pilot's rule of thumb is that if a Beaver still floats after loading, it will fly.

Beavers have seen service with over 60 countries, and in 29 of them they have been used as utility aircraft by the armed forces. The U.S. military purchased 968 Beavers as L-20As

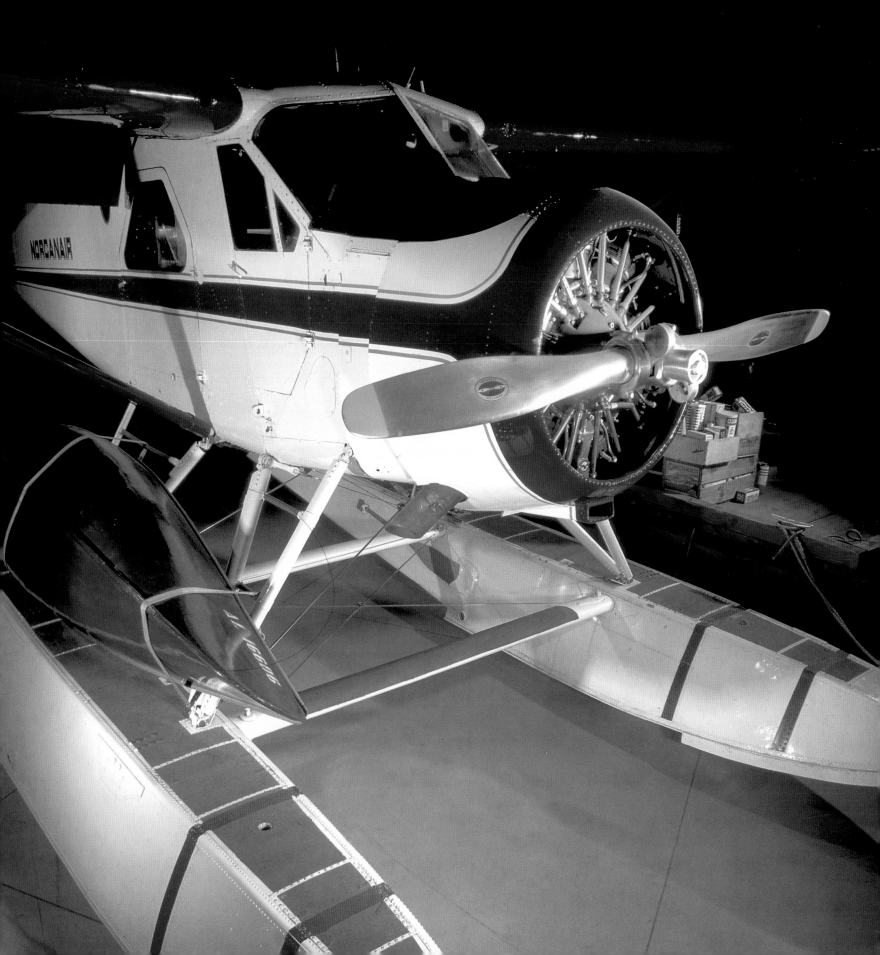

Kenmore Air in Seattle, Washington, operates a small airline in the Puget Sound region. They fly regularly scheduled air service from Seattle and up through the Sound are to Vancouver, Canada, all in floatplanes. The seven-passenger piston-engined Beaver is the mainstay of the Kenmore Fleet. Here, a Beaver slowly taxis away from the Kenmore Air Harbor at the north end of Lake Washington.

(until 1962 when they became U-6As) and a further six delivered as L-6Bs. This was the first peacetime U.S. purchase of a non-American built aircraft. Beavers saw service in both the Korean and Vietnam wars, where they were used for casualty evacuation, rescue, aerial photography, and courier services, as well as being cargo and personnel transports. The U.S. Navy's Test Pilot School still operates two DHC-2s to tow gliders and to instruct students in the evaluation of lateral-directional flying characteristics. A Royal New Zealand Air Force Beaver supported Sir Edmund Hillary's expedition to the South Pole.

Production finally ended in 1967, after 1,657 DHC-2 Beavers had been built. In a testament to their durability and utility, some two-thirds of the total Beavers constructed are still in use around the world, many modified to adapt to modern technology. The modifications completed by Kenmore Air of Seattle are so desirable in the aviation community that the rebuilt Beavers are identified as Kenmore Beavers. A modified 1950s Beaver that originally sold for under U.S. $50,000 can now fetch U.S. $500,000. Given its longevity, strength, versatility and popularity, it comes as no surprise that in 1987 the Beaver was named one of Canada's ten most important engineering achievements of the 20th century.

A Kenmore de Havilland Beaver flies over Lake Washington, downtown Seattle and the Space Needle barely visible through the haze.

D.H. Comet

Tragic Pioneer of the Jet Age

A SPECIFIC RECOMMENDATION OF BRITAIN'S wartime Brabazon Committee was for the development of a jet mailplane capable of carrying a ton of cargo across the Atlantic at 400 miles per hour. The initial proposal did not envisage the carriage of any passengers. However, by 1944 the parameters had changed to give priority to the provision of air services to the countries of Europe and the British Commonwealth. The range requirement was reduced to only 800 miles, and it was thought that the aircraft should have seats for 14 passengers. The company that took up the challenge of leading the way into the unknowns of the jet age for commercial aircraft, and then took several steps beyond the conservative concepts arising from the deliberations of the Brabazon Committee, was led by Sir Geoffrey de Havilland.

In 1946, de Havilland settled on a design for a four-jet, 32-seat airliner with gently swept wings. By the time of its first flight on July 27, 1949, the sleek D.H. 106 Comet 1 had become a breathtaking leap into aviation's future. It offered a cruising speed of 500 miles per hour at 40,000 feet, a range of 1,750 miles, and could seat up to 44 passengers. The skepticism of many in the airline industry about the economics of such an aircraft was swept aside soon after BOAC started flying the world's first jet passenger services between London and Johannesburg on May 2, 1952. Passengers loved the Comet for its smooth, quiet ride and for cutting journey times in half. The world's airlines paid attention and began lining up to place orders with de Havilland. The prestige of the British aircraft industry reached new heights, only to be dragged down by a series of horrific accidents.

John Cunningham was the de Havilland test pilot who flew the world's first jet airliner. Another portrait of Mr. Cunningham appears in the D.H. Mosquito chapter of this book on page 112. **Opposite:** The blended lines of the Comet are in evidence here. The embedded jet engines are a sign of a design decision not taken by Boeing in their competitive airline designs.

Perhaps the aircraft industry never received a greater shock than that of the mysterious losses of de Havilland Comet 1s in 1954. As the first jet airliner, the Comet was pioneering passenger-carrying operations at speeds and altitudes previously unknown to the airlines, and until 1954 it was a great success. The break-up of a Comet near Calcutta in 1953 was attributed to overstress in unusually severe weather conditions and therefore unlikely to be repeated. The picture began to change on January 10, 1954, when a BOAC Comet left Rome for London and climbed to 26,000 feet. At that point, the captain made a radio transmission that was never finished. Soon afterward, fishermen near the island of Elba saw wreckage plunging into the sea. The Comets were grounded while de Havilland and the British government investigated the disaster. Royal Navy divers and local fishermen did their best to recover as much of the aircraft as possible from 500 feet of water, and some 50 modifications were made to the rest of the Comet fleet in a speculative attempt to cover the problem. (The modifications included the installation of shields between the engines and fuel tanks, reinforced fuel lines and new smoke detectors.) With these completed, the Comets were cleared to fly again on March 23. The reprieve was short. On April 8, another Comet took off from Rome and disappeared during a climb to cruising altitude. Once more, Comets were grounded worldwide.

Meanwhile, some two-thirds of the Elba Comet had been recovered and techniques were being devised by the Royal Aircraft Establishment, Farnborough, that would set the pattern for all future investigations into major aircraft accidents. Thousands of

parts from the shattered Comet were painstakingly reassembled like a giant jigsaw and scrutinized for clues; forensic pathologists extracted crucial evidence from the bodies of the victims; and a giant tank was filled with water so that a Comet fuselage could be subjected to repeated pressure tests, simulating the effects of three hours of flight every ten minutes. When all the evidence was in, it became clear that the Comets had succumbed to metal fatigue. The Comet 1 was designed with square windows, and cracks had appeared at the corners, eventually leading to catastrophic failure of the pressurized fuselage, which exploded with great violence once a crack began to spread.

The de Havilland company paid a heavy price for pioneering jet transports. The only solution to the Comet's problem was a com-plete redesign including round windows. That took four years and led to the Comet 4, a much improved aircraft that could seat up to eighty passengers and had a range of 3,000 miles. It became the first jet airliner to fly a scheduled transatlantic service when BOAC inaugurated flights to New York on October 4, 1958, three weeks before PanAm began flying Boeing 707s to Paris. By then, however, it was too late for de Havilland to continue as the world's leader in jet travel. Paralleling the experience of the Wright brothers, once the concept was shown to be feasible, the baton of leadership slipped from the grasp of the pioneers and crossed the Atlantic, but this time in the opposite direction. Boeing was on the way to becoming the dominant force in the jet airliner industry.

Comet 4 G-APDA, seen here in BOAC markings. De Havilland paid a heavy price for pioneering jet transports, particularly in a series of crashes involving Comets 1s in 1954 that made obvious the need for a complete redesign. By the time the Comet 4 arrived in 1958, the Boeing 707 was well on its way to dominating the world's airliner business.

Above: Three of the revolutionary Comets in formation, before the tragedies that brought their domination of postwar air travel to a halt. Comet 1 G-ALYP is in the foreground, with G-ALVG and G-ALZK, the first and second prototypes, alongside. G-ALYP was the first Comet that disintegrated; it fell into the sea off the Italian coast in January of 1954. **Left:** The Comet 2, originally built as G-AMXF for British Overseas Airways Corporation, in RAF markings. Comet XK670 was later converted to C.Mk.2s specifications, fitted with strengthened freight doors, as were all 216 Comet 2s.

Vickers Viscount

Noble Turboprop

WHILE THEIR POSTWAR LARGE piston-engined airliners were generally abject failures, the United Kingdom's aircraft and engine manufacturers hoped for better things as they sought to take advantage of the running start Frank Whittle's genius had given them in the development of gas turbine technology. At this early stage in the history of the jet engine, neither the manufacturers nor the operators were entirely comfortable with the idea that pure jets were likely to be economically successful. The more cautious move toward adopting the new technology was to try the turboprop, in which the reassuring propeller was retained but was driven by a turbine. As passengers soon found, one advantage of this arrangement is that there are no reciprocating parts and therefore far less vibration than is produced by a piston engine.

The first turboprop to be used commercially was the Rolls-Royce Dart, four of which powered the aircraft on which Vickers banked its future, the Viscount. The original design resulted from the report of the Brabazon Committee calling for a smaller medium-range turboprop-powered pressurized aircraft to carry 24 passengers up to 1,750 miles at 200 miles per hour. British European Airways (BEA) was involved in the design and asked that the plane carry 32 passengers instead. At the same time, as insurance against failure, it was recommended that a piston-powered aircraft of similar performance should be produced. An order for two turboprop prototypes was placed with Vickers in March 1946, and construction started almost immediately.

The aircraft was provisionally named Viceroy, but the name was changed to Viscount after India gained its independence

The ubiquitous Vickers Viscount appears on these pages in just a few of the many livery that it flew under. Capital Airlines, later United, was the first U.S. operator of the Viscount. **Opposite:** British Airway's Viscount V 701, registration G-AMOG, now on display at RAF Museum Cosford. BEA, later BA, was formed in 1946 by an Act of Parliament, and operated European and North African routes from airports in the United Kingdom.

from Britain in 1947. The first prototype Viscount 630 made its initial flight in July 1948 and was awarded a restricted Certificate of Airworthiness on September 15, 1949. This was followed by a full certificate on July 27, 1950, and the Viscount was placed into service with BEA, the principal intended customer, the next day to familiarize the pilots and ground crew with the new aircraft.

The 32-seat Viscount 630 was then flown on route-proving trials, including the world's first scheduled turbine-powered service, which ran for a month between London and Paris from July 29, 1950. The conclusion drawn by BEA was that the design was too small and slow (275 miles per hour), making the per-passenger operating costs too high for regular service. As a result, an order was placed with Airspeed for 20 piston-engined Ambassadors.

At Vickers, the design team went back to the drawing board and produced the larger Type 700 Viscount, intended to carry up to 48 passengers and cruise at 308 miles per hour. The new prototype first flew on August 28, 1950. Although BEA had been less than enthusiastic about the Type 630, it had been noted that passengers reacted very favorably to turboprop travel. It was relatively quiet and smooth compared to flight powered by piston engines. When the stretched Viscount 701 arrived with more powerful Rolls-Royce Dart engines and 52 seats, BEA ordered 20. These entered regular airline service in April 1953, by which time Vickers was filling its order book. Sales started with Aer Lingus, Trans Canada, Trans Australia, and Air France. Significant sales were made in the United States, too, with 60 Viscounts going to Capital Airlines and another 15 to Continental.

Between October 8 and 10, 1953, BEA operated Viscount V.700 GA-MAV in the Transport Handicap section of the London-Christchurch Air Race; it flew the 12,365 miles in 40 hours, 43 minutes, calling at Bahrain, Colombo, Cocos Islands and Melbourne on the way. The average speed was 320 miles per hour and G-AMAV crossed the finish line nine hours ahead of its closest rival.

The final delivery and the 445th Viscount made, a series 800 aircraft stretched almost four feet and with seats for up to 71 passengers, went to All Nippon Airways in February 1963. The type continued in BEA and British Airways service until the 1980s, eventually being passed on to charter operators such as British Air Ferries (later British World). In 2004, three Viscounts were known to be still in service, all in Africa. By any standards, the Viscount can be judged a post-WWII aviation success and has a claim to being the aircraft which, more than any other, initiated the change in postwar air travel. That having been said, it is sobering to find that, of the 445 Viscounts delivered, 144 were destroyed in crashes in which 1,640 people died between August 1952 and April 2003. The most frequent critical factor mentioned in the crash reports is severe weather, but crew errors accounted for a number and several Viscounts were brought down by shoulder-fired missiles. One of the worst accidents occurred on July 24, 1992, when a Vickers 816 Viscount of Mandala Airlines flew into Lalaboy Mountain, Indonesia, at 2,300 feet while on an instrument approach to Ambon in a heavy rainstorm. None of the 70 people on board survived.

This Viscount V.794D, built for Turkish Airlines in 1958, was powered by Rolls-Royce Dart 510 turboprop engines. It had a brief service life and crashed on approach to Gatwick Airport south of London on February 17, 1959. The airliner was carrying Turkish Prime Minister Adnan Menderes, who survived the crash only to be hanged two years later following a military coup. Five of the crew of eight perished, as did nine of the sixteen passengers.

Continental Airlines originated in 1934 as Varney Speed Lines in the American southwest. In 1937 the name was changed to Continental Airlines.
After World War II, the airline began to expand its territory and in 1957 it flew for the first time from Chicago to Los Angeles.
Continental introduced turboprop service with the Vickers Viscount 800 Series, on the new medium-length routes.

BAC/Aerospatiale Concorde

Supersonic, at a Price

As the jet engine began to revolutionize air travel in the post WWII period, it seemed that there could be no limit to the advances it promised. Airliners would get bigger and safer, and would be able to reach across the globe, linking in hours countries that until then had been weeks apart. The dramatic increase in speed was immediately apparent, and it sparked an appetite for even faster travel. Military aircraft, ignoring economics, showed the way to supersonic flight, and as early as 1954 a group of British aerodynamicists began to study the possibility of building a supersonic airliner. It was no easy task. Overcoming the huge increase of drag occurring as the speed of sound is approached is only the start. There follow a multitude of problems, including those of the marked rise in surface heat produced by air friction. It was recognized that new alloys and design techniques would be required. In Britain, the Bristol 223 project was conceived as a four-engined delta capable of carrying 100 passengers from London to New York at Mach 2.

In 1960, Sud Aviation and Dassault in France formed a consortium to develop a Super Caravelle, originally intended to be a Mach 2.2, 76-seater for the transatlantic route. Since the costs of development were going to be high and the aviation industries of the two countries were pointed in the same direction, it seemed only sensible to join forces. By 1962 the French and British governments had signed an agreement whereby Aérospatiale and BAC would collaborate on the airframe while Rolls-Royce and SNECMA shared development of the Olympus 593 engines. The product of their joint efforts was the Concorde, an elegant delta with a wing leading edge shaped in a gentle S-curve. Plans to have

The Concorde taxis, revealing its spindly looking under-carriage, as well as the massive intakes for four Olympus engines, two on either side. No commercial aircraft was more controversial than the supersonic BAe-Aérospatial Concorde. Economically a failure, it was nevertheless an astonishing technological achievement.
Opposite: *Concorde* by Malcolm Root.

the aircraft in service by 1968 had seriously underestimated the difficulties (aerodynamic, structural and political) to be overcome, and it was not until March 1969 that the first prototype left the ground at Toulouse. The second flew from Filton, near Bristol, a month later.

Aérospatiale and BAC might have hoped that their immensely costly project would at last bring its rewards, but it was not to be. With the oil crisis of the 1970s bringing fears of finite fuel reserves, and more commercially viable alternatives available, those airlines that had taken options on Concorde did not renew them. Spectacular demonstrations of the aircraft's performance (including one in which an Air France Concorde accomplished a round-trip between Boston and Paris before a 747 completed a direct flight) drew international applause but did nothing for sales. In 1974, in the absence of further orders, it was agreed that production would be stopped after British Airways and Air France had each received seven aircraft. On January 21, 1976, 14 years after the Anglo-French agreement was signed, Concorde at last entered commercial service, British Airways flying from London to Bahrein and Air France linking Paris and Buenos Aires. The rich prize of North Atlantic services had to wait until May 1976, after a U.S. government environmental study had opened the way for flights to Washington, DC.

Until the summer of 2000, British Airways and Air France continued to fly Concordes both on regular scheduled services and on charter flights. The transatlantic service, offering crossings of only three to three and a half hours, was immensely popular with the rich and famous. Those fortunate enough to be able to

afford the fare used Concorde often and were unstinting in their praise, claiming that the rapidity of the crossing effectively removed the problem of fatigue. For a quarter of a century, Concorde reigned supreme as an aeronautical phenomenon, an aerial high-speed yacht for the rich, admired and desired as unobtainable by most of the traveling public. The achievement of British and French designers and engineers was remarkable and remained unmatched in the 20th century, a collaborative technological triumph that did wonders for Anglo-French prestige. Pilots loved it, too. British Airways' chief of Concorde Flight Operations, Captain Mike Bannister, has said: "Concorde handles so beautifully she's more like a thoroughbred race horse or a sports car than a truck. All the pilots that fly her take great delight in the physical part of flying the aeroplane." He added: "The first time you do a takeoff in training where you use full power but the aircraft is only about 60 percent of its maximum weight, the acceleration is quite spectacular. You can get from a standing start to airborne at 250 miles per hour in about 20 seconds, and to 3,000 feet in about 35 seconds. For an airliner that is quite remarkable." Remarkable it was, but there is no doubting that Concorde was a commercial disaster. Between them, the British and French taxpayers paid some one and a half billion dollars to put a handful of inefficient aircraft into service for the benefit of very few privileged people.

On July 25, 2000, a wheel of an Air France Concorde, taking off from Charles de Gaulle airport near Paris, struck a loose strip of metal on the runway just before aircraft rotation. Pieces of rubber flew off and struck the underside of the left wing. Fire broke out as fuel gushed from a ruptured fuel tank and the aircraft got airborne trailing flames. Soon afterwards, the crew were faced with control difficulties that proved impossible to overcome. Less than a minute after the nosewheel burst, the Concorde crashed into a small hotel, killing all 109 people on board plus four more on the ground. All Concordes were grounded pending modifications and the reissuing of Certificates of Airworthiness by the British and French authorities. They returned to service only briefly before their final retirement in October 2003, a little less than 28 years after they began blazing the trail of supersonic travel.

On final approach, the Concorde turns humid air into visible condensation. Also visible, the drooping nose of the airliner, designed to be lowered when the sleek airliner is operating at slower speeds and to increase the view from the cockpit.

Above: Above the clouds, four of the British Airway's Concordes in a rare formation. Until the summer of 2000, British Airways and Air France continued to fly Concordes both on regularly scheduled flights and on charter flights. The transatlantic service offered crossings of only three to three and a half hours. **Right:** The cramped cockpit of the Concorde. Flying the supersonic airliner was an exercise in systems management, because the balance of the aircraft constantly changes as the fuel is burned off. Aeronautical engineers, pilots and passengers who could afford the fare loved it; accountants and those who lived near its takeoff flight paths hated it.

Flying Club Cessnas

Why Drive When You Can Fly?

CLYDE CESSNA DIED IN NOVEMBER 1954 at age 74 after spending most of his life in the aviation business. He never held a pilot's license and had a rudimentary education, but he was driven to succeed in whatever he turned his hand to and he was a genius when it came to flying machines.

Until 1911, Cessna sold cars in Enid, Oklahoma, but he was fascinated by the story of Louis Blériot's flight across the English Channel in 1909. At the age of 31 he built a copy of Blériot's Type XI that he called *Silverwing*. On the plain near Jet, Oklahoma, he taught himself to fly, suffering many accidents in the process. His perseverance was rewarded in December 1911 when he made a successful 5-mile flight near Enid that included turns and a safe landing. Cessna now enjoyed a period of exhibition flying, but during the years 1912 to 1915 he built several monoplanes, and discovered that what he really wanted to do was manufacture and sell aircraft of his own design.

In 1916, Cessna took over a vacant building in Wichita, Kansas, and built a new aircraft for the 1917 season. He also established a flight school, but the U.S. intervention in WWI brought his enterprise to an end and he became a farmer for a few years. His interest in aeronautics never waned, however, and he flew a Laird Swallow during the early 1920s. In 1924, Cessna was approached by Lloyd Stearman and Walter Beech, who were planning to start a new business to be known as the Travel Air Manufacturing Company and wanted Cessna to join them. In return for his agreement, he was named president. Travel Air produced several excellent aircraft in the next two years, but in 1927 Cessna broke away to form the Cessna Aircraft Company. Between 1927 and

A lineup of Cessna twin engines. Flying the push-pull Skymaster, with the engines inline, does not qualify a pilot for a multi-engine certificate, as major requirements are single-engine operations and dealing with non-symmetrical thrust issues. **Opposite:** The venerable Cessna 182 RG Skylane will fly long distances at a reasonable fuel per hour rate. RG stands for retractable landing gear. The pilot of this aircraft must have a complex aircraft rating.

1929, the company marketed a succession of four- and six-seat monoplanes, but the Wall Street collapse in 1929 brought Cessna the prospect of bankruptcy, and in 1931 the board of Cessna Aircraft voted to oust Clyde Cessna and close the factory. Undaunted, he rented facilities in the abandoned Travel Air complex and created the C.V. Cessna Aircraft Co., which specialized in building racing aircraft. In 1933, however, Cessna was dealt another blow when his close friend Roy Liggett died in the crash of the CR-2 racer. A grief-stricken Cessna withdrew from aviation and retreated to his farm.

In 1934, Cessna's nephew Dwane Wallace wrested control of the defunct Cessna Aircraft Company from the stockholders and introduced the Cessna C-34 monoplane. Clyde agreed to participate in the new venture only as a figurehead. The C-34 was a success and was named the world's most efficient light aircraft. Wallace guided the company through the 1930s and oversaw the development of the T-50, which became the Cessna Bobcat of WWII. With the end of the war, a boom was forecast in the U.S. private aviation industry. It proved to be a self-fulfilling prophecy — for a while. In 1946, there was a bustle of activity, with the impressive total of over 31,000 light planes built. The overproduction was serious, however, and a rash of failures and mergers followed a collapse in demand. By 1948, total industry production was down to little more than 7,000. At this low volume of production it was impossible to keep prices down and the idea of private flying for everyone faded.

The "Big Three" survivors of the postwar mayhem were Cessna, Beech and Piper. Wallace introduced the classic taildragger Cessna

Left: The familiar front cowling of the Cessna family of single-engine aircraft. A Cessna 170 would have had a base price of $5,400 in 1948.
In May 1972, Cessna became the first manufacturer to exceed a total production of 100,000 aircraft. As many as half the aircraft flying in the world today
are Cessnas. **Right:** Before the Cessna 182 came the 180, and it remains one of the greatest private aircraft ever built.
Powerful and with a rugged tailwheel configuration, the 180 can operate from short and rough airstrips.

Model 190/195, and launched the Model 120/140, founding a line that would grow to dominate the light aircraft market and become a familiar sight at flying clubs the world over. The growth of the Big Three was marked by their continually improving products. Cessna rolled on through higher and higher model numbers — 150, 170 (1948 base price $5,400), 172 Skyhawk, 175 Skylark, 180, 182, and 185 Skylane. In May 1972 the success of these machines was evidenced when Cessna became the first manufacturer to exceed a total production of 100,000 aircraft.

In the 1980s the light aircraft industry went rapidly downhill, and one particularly significant reason for the decline in the United States was the problem of product liability. Insurance became a necessity, markedly increasing production costs. By the late 1980s, the effects of litigation had helped to almost double the price of each aircraft built. Independent operation became difficult for even large companies to sustain, and Cessna was made a subsidiary of General Dynamics in 1985, at the same time suspending single-engine production "until the product liability

laws are reformed." In 1992 Cessna changed allegiance again when it was bought by Textron. Some relief came in 1994 when the General Aviation Revitalization Act came into effect in the U.S., establishing an 18-year statute of repose against makers of general aviation aircraft and parts. Cessna announced its return, and by the late 1990s the company's popular high-wing single-engine models were back in production. The Cessna 172 Skyhawk was among those that reappeared, suitably updated but still recognizable as the descendant of the original 172 manufactured almost 50 years before. It was one of the most successful aircraft designs ever conceived; by the end of the century over 37,000 individuals of the Skyhawk family had been built. This extraordinary achievement reflects the dominance of both Cessna and the United States generally in the field of general aviation. Some 80 percent of the world's general aviation aircraft are in the U.S., and Cessna has built a total of more than 180,000 aircraft of all models. It has been estimated that perhaps half of the aircraft being flown in the world are from a Cessna factory.

A 1950s Cessna family portrait. Big brother Cessna 310 watches over a 175 and two 182As. Swept-back fins began appearing in 1960. The Cessna 310 was the first twin-engine aircraft design from Cessna to enter production after World War II. The sleek modern lines of the new twin were backed up by innovative features such as the storage of all fuel in tip tanks in early models.

Learjet

The Businessman's Aerial Hotrod

THE BUSINESS EXECUTIVE AIRCRAFT really came into its own when it was fitted with small jet engines. Here was the ultimate symbol of corporate success, a machine that could soar above the common herd of commercial airliners, carrying its well-heeled passengers directly to their chosen destinations at high subsonic speeds in pampered luxury. De Havilland in Britain and Dassault in France both showed interest in developing small business jets. The D.H.125 began taking shape in 1959, but did not fly until 1962, by when the company had merged with the Hawker Siddeley group, so the aircraft was sold as the H.S.125, and later, after a further merger produced British Aerospace, as the BAe.125. In France, the Dassault company took the wing of its celebrated Mystère fighter and designed a business jet fuselage to mount it on. The result was the Mystère Falcon 20, the forerunner of a perennially successful line.

At least one businessman thought that the 125s and Falcons were too grandiose by far. Bill Lear described them scornfully as the modern equivalent of "royal barges," and set out to produce something more practical. Lear was an unusual genius. He dropped out of high school after six weeks, worked odd jobs, learned to fly and started working on inventions that eventually earned him more than 150 patents, ranging from the first autopilot for a jet aircraft to the eight-track tape player to the first brushless electric motor. He made and lost fortunes four times in his life, and collected several honorary degrees along the way. In the mid-1950s, he became intrigued by the Swiss FFA P-16 fighter project, and was inspired to establish the Swiss American Aircraft Corporation in 1960 with the aim of manufacturing a relatively simple high-speed executive jet, less costly to buy and

When the prototype Learjet made its first flight in October 1963, it was the first of what has become an enormous industry, the business jet. The aircraft's slim, rakish good looks caught the public imagination like no other. **Opposite:** The Learjet 24 was the first business jet to be certified. This model evolved through several variations and total of 259 were built.

operate than any then on the market. A smaller fuselage was at the heart of his design. His argument was that people did not stand up in cars, and they need not do so when traveling by air, so headroom was unnecessary. When it made its appearance in 1963 at the new Lear Jet Industries company facility in Wichita, the Learjet prototype's slim, rakish good looks caught the public imagination like no other.

In no time at all, the name Learjet became the term popularly used for executive jets generally, whatever their origins. Highly visible figures from the entertainment world, including Frank Sinatra, were early customers. In 1974, the worldwide Learjet fleet had exceeded one million flight hours and in 1975 the company produced its 500th jet. In both instances they were the first manufacturer to reach that mark. By late 1976, the company had increased the number of aircraft being produced each month to ten. That same year, golfer Arnold Palmer used a Learjet 36 to put his name into the aviation record books, completing a 20,000 mile round-the-world flight in less than fifty-seven and a half hours.

Bill Lear had moved on to other things in 1969, after Gates Rubber acquired a controlling interest in his company, but the new owners kept the name and continued to develop the aircraft. However, Bill Lear's fertile imagination was still in high gear when he left Lear Jet. He began work on another business jet, the Learstar 600, a design which was taken over in 1976 by Canadair and became the Challenger. When it first flew in November 1978, the Challenger brought widebody comfort to executive aviation and was immediately popular on that account. In 1986, Bombardier, a Canadian industrial company, acquired Canadair and then in 1990 both lines initiated by Bill Lear came together when Gates

A lineup of Learjet 23s. The design of this model was based on that of a Swiss strike-fighter project. Bill Lear was an unusual genius who made and lost fortunes four times in his life. His aim with the Learjet was to manufacture a relatively simple high-speed executive jet that would be less costly to buy than any then on the market. A smaller fuselage was key to his design. He reasoned that people did not stand up while riding in cars, so why should they do anything other than sit while flying?

sold Lear Jet to Bombardier also. Challenger development has continued and the Learjet family has gone on to retain a solid share of the lighter executive jet market. The Learjet 31 and 45 both possess Learjet's legendary performance, leaping off the ground like fighters and climbing to altitudes as high as 51,000 feet.

On one occasion, the ability of business jets to fly at heights above most airliner traffic proved disastrous. On October 25, 1999, golfer Payne Stewart and several others (Jerri Gibbs of Leader Enterprises, Orlando; Robert Fraley and Van Ardan, Payne Stewart's agents; and the pilots, Michael Kling and Stephanie Bellegarrigue) were flying in a Lear Jet 35 from Orlando, Florida to Dallas, Texas. A loss of cabin pressure was not detected by the flight crew. Jacksonville's Air Traffic Control Center attempted to make contact and got no response. USAF F-16s shadowed the aircraft for three hours at heights above 40,000 feet as it continued to fly on autopilot until all fuel was exhausted. It is estimated that all aboard were dead from hypoxia before the plane left Florida's radar. The aircraft crashed near Mina, South Dakota.

Learjet N505PF was the sixth Learjet built. In the 1960s the name Learjet became the term popularly used for executive jets, whatever their origins.

X-15

Rocketing into Space

THE NORTH AMERICAN X-15 was the most remarkable of the rocket research aircraft. It was missile-shaped and 50 feet long, with a wedge-shaped fin and thin wings spanning only 22 feet. The X-15 had its first, unpowered glide flight launched from a B-52 at 37,550 feet on June 8, 1959, and the first powered flight followed on September 17, 1959. On both occasions it was flown by test pilot Scott Crossfield. From 1955 to 1961, Crossfield was the design specialist, X-15 project pilot, and chief engineering test pilot for North American Aviation. While flying the initial series of tests, he achieved a speed of Mach 2.97 and an altitude of 88,116 feet. Shortly after launch on his third flight, a rocket engine exploded. Unable to jettison his propellants, Crossfield had to attempt an overweight landing. During the rapid descent, the cockpit windows frosted over and Crossfield was flying blind. Ever resourceful, he used one of his socks to wipe clear a peephole so that he could see and be guided to a landing by the mission chase plane. On touchdown, the excessive load broke the aircraft's back, but Crossfield was uninjured and the aircraft was eventually repaired.

The North American Aviation-built rocket plane is launched from the B-52 mothership. Carried to 45,000 feet, the X-15 then dropped away and the rockets were fired. **Opposite:** The X-15A at the National Museum of the USAF was flown by Major "Pete" Knight to Mach 6.72 on October 3, 1967. The 22-foot-long fuel tanks were carried alongside the fuselage, one containing anhydrous ammonia and the other liquid oxygen. The contents of these tanks weighed almost 16 tons, and was burned by the X-15A in two and a half minutes.

On June 8, 1960, Crossfield had another close call during ground tests with the XLR-99 rocket engine. He was seated in the cockpit of X-15-3 when a malfunctioning valve caused a catastrophic explosion. His description of the event belittled what must have been horrifying experience: "It was a pretty violent activity for a moment or two. It was like being inside the sun. It was such a fire outside that it was a very brilliant orange. The fore part of the airplane, which was all that was left, was blown about thirty feet forward, and I was in it. Of course I was pretty safe because I was in a structure that was designed to resist the very high temperatures of reentry flight." Once again he emerged unscathed. On December 6, he completed his fourteenth and final flight in the X-15, so ending North American's demonstration program.

The X-15 was developed to provide in-flight information and data on aerodynamics, structures, flight controls, and the physiological aspects of high-speed, high-altitude flight. A wealth of data was gathered on hypersonic air flow, aerodynamic heating, control and stability at hypersonic speeds, reaction controls for flight above the atmosphere, piloting techniques for reentry, human factors, and flight instrumentation. For flight within the Earth's atmosphere, the X-15 used conventional aerodynamic controls, but outside the atmosphere, a reaction control system was used. Thrusters located on the nose of the aircraft provided pitch and yaw control, while those on the wings controlled roll. The X-15 weighed about 14,000 pounds empty and close to 34,000 pounds at launch. The Thiokol XLR-99 rocket engine was pilot controlled and was capable of developing 57,000 pounds of thrust. Thrust was available for the first 80 to 120 seconds of flight. The remainder of the 10- to 11-minute flight was without power and ended with a 200-mph glide landing.

Only twelve test pilots flew the X-15. Among them was Robert White, who in 1961 became the first man to exceed Mach 4, Mach 5 and Mach 6. On July 17, 1962, he took the X-15 to a record-setting altitude of 314,750 feet, more than 59 miles above the Earth's surface, so qualifying for astronaut wings. As he described it afterward: "My flights to 217,000 feet and 314,750

USAF Major General Joe Engle flew the X-15 sixteen times, three of them exceeding an altitude of 50 miles, which is the altitude that qualifies a pilot for astronaut rating. He went on to fly the space shuttle and has logged over 224 hours in space.

feet were very dramatic in revealing the Earth's curvature…at my highest altitude I could turn my head through a 180-degree arc and wow! — the Earth is really round." President Kennedy later presented the Collier Trophy jointly to White and three of his fellow X-15 pilots, NASA's Joseph Walker, Forrest Peterson of the U.S. Navy, and Scott Crossfield.

After graduating from the Air Force Experimental Test Pilot School in 1961 and the Air Force Aerospace Research Pilot School in 1962, Joe Engle became an X-15 test pilot. He piloted the aircraft on 16 flights and three times reached altitudes of more than 50 miles, thereby becoming the nation's youngest astronaut. In the late 1950s, "Pete" Knight was involved in the advanced testing of the F-100 Super Sabre, and in 1960 was one of five pilots selected for the development of the X-20 Dyna Soar. After the X-20 was canceled, Knight joined the X-15 test program. On October 3, 1967, he flew X-15A-2 on a flight designed to "push the edge of the envelope." High over the Mojave Desert, his aircraft dropped away from the B-52 and he ignited the rocket engine to

begin his climb. As the outboard propellants burned out, he jettisoned the two external fuel tanks and hurtled forward through the thin atmosphere, leveling off at just over 100,000 feet. Boosted by over 140 seconds of engine-burn time, the X-15 accelerated to Mach 6.7, the highest speed ever achieved in a manned aircraft other than the Space Shuttle. During this flight, the aircraft surface temperature exceeded 3000 degrees Fahrenheit.

Flying the X-15 was undoubtedly a hazardous and challenging business, but only one of the test pilots was killed during the program. On November 15, 1967, X-15-3 crashed, resulting in the death of Michael J. Adams. The aircraft began to spin on the descent and disintegrated when the forces on the machine reached 15 G, scattering wreckage over 50 square miles.

Three X-15s were built, and over a period of almost ten years, they made 199 test flights, the last one on October 24, 1968. The X-15-1 can be seen at the National Air and Space Museum, Washington DC, and X-15A-2 is at the National Museum of the United States Air Force, Dayton, Ohio.

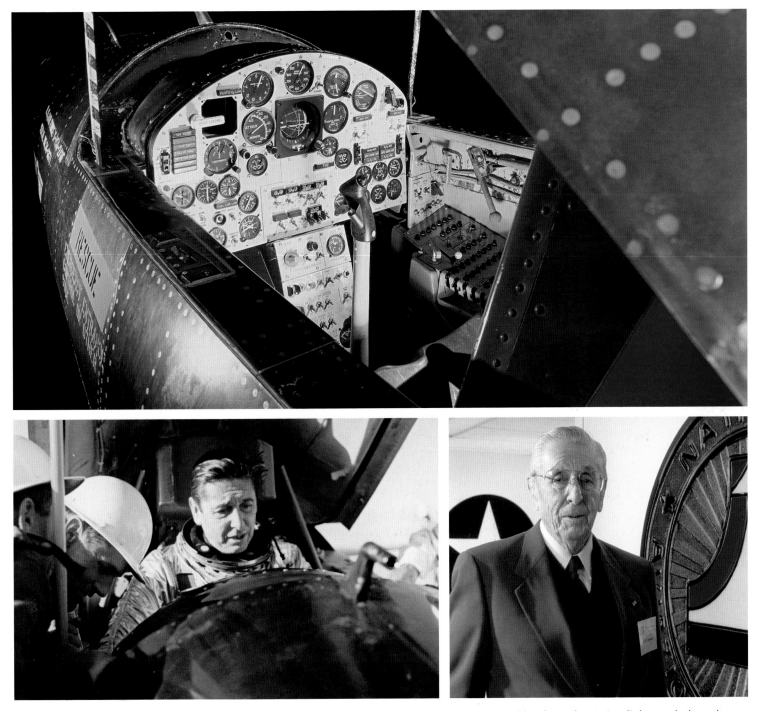

Top: The relatively simple cockpit of the X-15A. The instrument dials are nearly outnumbered by the red warning lights and placards.
Bottom Left: Scott Crossfield in the cockpit of the X-15. On November 20, 1953, he became the first man to fly at twice the speed of sound as he piloted the Douglas Skyrocket to a speed of 1,291 miles per hour (Mach 2.005). He was deeply involved in the design and proving of the rocket plane, and became the test pilot for North American Aviation. **Bottom Right:** Scott Crossfield, a 1983 enshrinee of the National Aviation Hall of Fame, photographed at their facility in 2000.

SR-71

High-Speed Blackbird

As TENSIONS ROSE IN THE early days of the Cold War, attempts were made to remove the risk from strategic reconnaissance. The search was on for aircraft of such high performance that they could operate anywhere in the world with impunity. Martin RB-57s performed in the role for a while, and then came two remarkable aircraft from Lockheed's "Skunk Works." The first, the U-2, looked like a jet-powered sailplane. Even in its earliest form, the U-2 could operate up to 70,000 feet, and that seemed to put them out of reach of the Soviets. In the late 1950s, overflights of the Soviet Union gained invaluable information about such things as bomber deployment, air defense systems and submarine development. However, on May 1, 1960, a U-2 flown by Francis Gary Powers was shot down near Sverdlovsk by SA-2 missiles. Chairman Kruschev used the incident to embarrass President Eisenhower, and penetrations of Soviet airspace were brought to a halt, at least for the time being. At Lockheed, the Skunk Works was already at work on an aircraft capable of presenting the Soviets with a greater challenge. By the mid-1960s, the U.S. had the SR-71 Blackbird, a strategic reconnaissance vehicle that could match the U-2's performance for range and altitude while adding the ability to sustain flight at more than three times the speed of sound.

The precursor of the SR-71 was the Lockheed A-12, designed for the CIA by Kelly Johnson. The first flight took place at Groom Lake, Nevada, on April 25, 1962. This was an aircraft initially designated A-11 since it was fitted with Pratt & Whitney J75s rather than the more powerful J58s intended but not yet available. Thirteen A-12s were built, and they gave rise to several similar

The "Blackbird" in its mysterious glory on an airbase tarmac somewhere, attended by equally mysterious crews. The pressure suits and helmets are for very high-altitude operations.
Opposite: Kelly Johnson and his design colleagues at Lockheed's "Skunk Works" created an otherworldly shape in the SR-71. It remains one of the highest performing aircraft in history, even now over 40 years after the first flights.

aircraft, variously designated M-21 (2 built), YF-12A (3), SR-71A (29), SR-71B (2), and SR-71C (1). Of these 50 aircraft, 20 were lost in accidents, 12 of which were SR-71s. The USAF's reconnaissance version was originally called the R-12, but when a strike capability became an option it became RS-71 (Reconnaissance Strike). However, then USAF Chief of Staff Curtis LeMay preferred SR-71, giving the strike role pride of place. Before the Blackbird was revealed to the public in a speech by President Johnson on February 29, 1964, LeMay insisted on modifying the text to read SR-71. The media transcript given to the press still had the earlier RS-71 designation, and so it was assumed that the president had misread the plane's designation.

The public disclosure of the aircraft and its designation came as a shock to everyone at Lockheed's "Skunk Works" and to the USAF personnel involved in the program. All of the Maintenance Manuals, Flight Crew Handbooks, training slides still referred to the aircraft as R-12. Following President Johnson's speech, the designation change was taken as an order from the Commander-in-Chief, and immediate republishing began of new materials retitled SR-71.

Although the A-12 first flew in 1962, the first SR-71 did not enter service with the 4200th (later 9th) Strategic Reconnaissance Wing at Beale Air Force Base, California, until January 1966. On March 21, 1968, Major (later General) Jerome F. O'Malley and Major Edward D. Payne flew the first operational SR-71 sortie in SR-71 serial number 64-17976. During its career, this aircraft (976) accumulated 2,981 flying hours and flew 942 sorties, including 257 operational missions, from Beale AFB; Palmdale,

Right: On March 21, 1968, in the aircraft on display, Major (later General) Jerome F. O'Malley and Major Edward D. Payne made the first operational SR-71 sortie, over Vietnam. During its career, this aircraft accumulated 2,981 flying hours and flew 942 total sorties (more than any other SR-71), including 257 operational missions, from Beale Air Force Base, California, Palmdale, California, Kadena Air Base, Okinawa, and RAF (Base) Mildenhall, England. **Below:** Tom Allison, seen here in front of Al Williams' *Gulfhawk.* Before he became the Head of the Collection Division at the National Air and Space Museum, his career in the USAF included flying the Blackbird.

California; Kadena Air Base, Okinawa, Japan; and RAF Mildenhall, England. The aircraft was flown to the United States Air Force Museum near Dayton, Ohio, in March 1990.

One remarkable variant of the A-12 was the M-21. This aircraft was modified by adding a second cockpit for a launch control officer. The M-21 was equipped to carry the D-21, an unmanned, faster and higher flying reconnaissance drone. Once the D-21 drone was launched, it was planned that it would overfly the target, travel to a rendezvous point and eject its data package. The package would be recovered in midair by a C-130 Hercules and the drone would self destruct. The program was canceled in 1966 after a flight during which the launching aircraft's shockwave held the drone back and it crashed into the M-21's tailplane. The crew survived the midair collision but the launch control officer drowned when he opened his helmet after landing in the ocean and his flight suit filled with water. The surviving M-21 is on display, with a D-21B drone, at the Museum of Flight in Seattle, Washington.

The SR-71 remained the world's fastest and highest-flying operational manned aircraft throughout its career. From an altitude of 80,000 feet it could survey 100,000 square miles of the Earth's surface per hour. On July 28, 1976, an SR-71 recorded an absolute speed record of 2,193 miles per hour and reached an altitude of 85,069 feet in sustained flight. When the SR-71 was first retired in 1990, one was flown from Palmdale, California, to Washington, DC, in 64 minutes, setting a coast-to-coast record at an average speed of 2,124 miles per hour. On September 1, 1974, an SR-71 also set the record for flying from New York to London in one hour and 55 minutes. (Commercial Concorde flights took around three hours, 20 minutes, and Boeing 747s average twice as long as that.)

The U.S. Air Force retired its fleet of SR-71s on January 26, 1990, temporarily reactivated some of them in 1995 and began flying operational missions again in January 1997. They were retired permanently in 1998.

Don Watkins and Bob Fowlkes flew SR-71 61-7976 to the National Museum of the USAF at Wright-Patterson AFB on March 27, 1990.

MiG-21

Flying Fishbed

HAVING SURPRISED THE WEST with the MiG-15 in 1947, the wizards of the Soviet aviation industry went on pulling jet-powered rabbits out of their hats. The Mikoyan-Gurevich factory improved the basic breed with the MiG-17 Fresco and the supersonic MiG-19 Farmer, before moving on to the astonishingly successful (and relatively cheap) delta-winged MiG-21 Fishbed in the late 1950s. The E-5 prototype of the MiG-21 was first flown in 1955 and made its public appearance during the Soviet Aviation Day display at Moscow's Tushino Airport in June 1956.

A specification based on the experience of air combat during the Korean War was issued for a new Soviet fighter in 1953. The Mikoyan design team's submission was for a compact supersonic aircraft powered by a single afterburning turbojet. It was not intended for use in many different roles. The basic requirement was for an interceptor that could shoot down the USAF's B-52 and B-58 bombers. It had to be very fast (Mach 2 plus), maneuverable, and able to reach altitudes in excess of 50,000 feet quickly. These parameters were not compatible with heavy loads of fuel, electronics or weapons. It was accepted that initially the fighter would be used in the point defense role, would have gun armament only, and would operate under close ground control.

As a result of these restrictions, when the MiG-21 was first introduced it had a number of built-in shortcomings, but the design was one that proved capable of considerable development as time passed. By 1960 the MiG-21F-13 was in mass production. Though its pilots said it was a delightful aircraft to fly, with no handling vices, excellent all-round performance and good maneuverability,

Polish aviation photographer Mariusz Adamski captured this dead-ahead view of the MiG-21, which emphasizes the thin wings and nearly all-engine shape of the fuselage.
Opposite: The intake for the MiG-21's Tumansky turbojet includes a fixed conical center-body containing the airborne intercept radar.

it was still suffering from serious limitations. The fuel could not all be used without running into stability problems. This meant that it was virtually impossible to accelerate to the theoretically attainable level speed of Mach 2 because too much fuel would be used in the process. No search radar was fitted and armament was just two close-range missiles and one gun with 75 rounds.

The early MiG-21's AA-2 air-to-air missiles were not very effective, and the gyro gunsight could be thrown off target by high-speed maneuvers. These problems were progressively remedied as a result of experience in the Arab/Israeli and Vietnam wars and the MiG-21 eventually became an effective combat aircraft. During the Vietnam War, however, North Vietnamese pilots who had flown the MiG-17 were not at first keen to accept the MiG-21, which had a high wing-loading and consequently was not as agile as its predecessor. However, 13 North Vietnamese MiG-21 pilots claimed more than five aerial victories and attained ace status during the war.

Nguyen Van Coc was the most successful North Vietnamese ace with nine USAF kills claimed (seven confirmed by U.S. sources — three F-4s, three F-105s, and one F-102A). On August 23, 1967, two MiG-21s of the 91st Fighter Regiment, VPAF, intercepted a USAF raid. The size of the USAF formation (forty aircraft,) encouraged the U.S. crews to feel that they would not be troubled by fighters. Suddenly, one F-4D crew, Charles Tyler (pilot) and Ronald Sittner (WSO) of the 8th Tactical Fighter Wing, heard an F-105D pilot (Elmo Baker) calling that he had been hit by a MiG-21's missile and was ejecting. As Tyler looked for the enemy, an explosion shook his

Photographer Adamski caught this Polish Air Force MiG-21 MF Fishbed-J above the clouds. Over 11,000 of these fighters were produced and flown by the air forces of over 50 countries.

aircraft. He ejected after control was lost. Tyler and Baker were captured by North Vietnamese troops as soon as they reached the ground. Sittner had been killed in the explosion. Both aircraft had been shot down by Atoll missiles fired from MiG-21s flown by Nguyen Van Coc and Nguyen Nhat Chieu. Two more F-4Ds were shot down during the engagement without loss to the MiGs. It was one of the VPAF's better days.

The Indian Air Force was one of the largest users of the MiG-21. The Indians were swift to recognize that the lack of the guns and the poor reliability of the Atoll missiles were major shortcomings of the MiG-21PF they were acquiring, so they asked for a gun-pack to be added to the aircraft. This proved to be a wise decision during the final days of the 1971 war between India and Pakistan. On December 12, an IAF MiG-21 launched an Atoll missile at a PAF F-104 that had attacked Jamnagar Air Base. The F-104 evaded,

firing flares to deflect the missile. The MiG-21 pilot then selected guns and fired three short bursts from about 300 yards. The F-104 burst into flame and the pilot ejected. This was the first supersonic air combat in South Asia, and the first of three victories scored against PAF F-104As using MiG-21 gunpacks.

The other major user was China, where a locally built MiG-21 derivative, the J-7, was produced. First introduced to service in 1965, the J-7 was steadily improved and was still in production at the end of the century. The MiG-21 was also exported widely elsewhere and was operated well past the time where it might have been considered obsolete. While technologically inferior to later fighter designs, its low production and maintenance costs made it a favorite of many nations. Over 11,000 MiG-21s and derivatives were built, more that any other jet fighter—and it served in the air forces of almost 50 nations.

Right: Two Polish Navy MiG-21bis in formation with three German Navy Tornados. This formation of former opposites is remarkable in that just a few years earlier it was beyond the imagination of the "Cold Warriors" on both sides of the Iron Curtain. Poland is now a member of NATO and joint exercises are common. **Below:** More than 50 countries of the world, including those friendly to the United States, have flown the MiG-21. At least 15 versions of the MiG-21 have been produced, some outside the Soviet Union. Estimates place the number built at more than 11,000, a production total exceeding that of any other modern jet aircraft. The MiG-21F shown here appears to have been built in Czechoslovakia and to have flown in the air force of that nation. It is painted and marked as a MiG-21PF of the North Vietnamese Air Force during the Vietnam War.

F-4 Phantom II

The Rhino

THE MOST OBVIOUS CANDIDATE for the title of dominant combat aircraft of the 1960s and 1970s was the McDonnell Douglas F-4 Phantom II, sometimes known to its crews as the Rhino because of its long snout and rugged exterior. With its bent-up wingtips, anhedral tailplane, big boundary-layer plates for the engine intakes, and slab-sided fuselage, the F-4 appeared to be a collection of fixes hastily assembled to solve unexpected aerodynamic problems. However, its considerable bulk was hauled along by two powerful J-79 engines, giving rise to the comment that even a brick would fly if it was given enough thrust. Even while such unkind observations were being made, they were quickly overshadowed by the Phantom's awesome performance.

Originally thought of simply as a fleet air defense fighter to replace the Demon, the F-4's exceptional capabilities soon led it to be employed in other roles — air superiority, interdiction, close support, photo-reconnaissance — and by other services. The first major in-service variant was the F-4B, which joined Squadron VF-101 of the U.S. Navy in 1961, but the Phantom II had begun to attract the attention of the aviation world before that with a series of records, among them an altitude of 98,557 feet in December 1959, a 500-kilometer closed circuit flown at 1,217 miles per hour, and a 100-kilometer closed circuit at 1,390 miles per hour in September 1960. The record-breaking continued with a world speed record of 1,606 miles per hour in November 1961, and an altitude of 98,425 feet was reached in just six minutes, 11 seconds, in April 1962. In May 1961, the Phantoms of VF-101 smashed John Glenn's transcontinental F8U record by flying from Los Angeles to New York in two hours,

The Phantom II is all awkward angles and brute power. Over Vietnam, Phantoms scored 145 kills. **Opposite:** Looking straight down the nose of the McDonnell-Douglas Phantom II on display at the National Museum of the USAF. The F-4 Phantom II was the most significant Western combat aircraft to appear in the 1960s. It made its mark in air superiority, strike and reconnaissance roles as well as specialized "Wild Weasel" anti-aircraft missile suppression missions.

47 minutes, an average of 870 miles per hour, and they did it while carrying missiles and external fuel tanks. This extraordinary multirole fighting machine was so good that it outdid its more specialized counterparts at their own game and challenged airmen everywhere to rethink their ideas about how best to fight the air war. The Phantom II quickly established itself as the world's most effective combat aircraft and besides becoming the predominant type used by the U.S. Navy and Marine Corps it was seized upon by the USAF and flown by the air forces of a dozen other countries, including the United Kingdom, Germany, Japan, Israel, Iran, Greece, Turkey, Spain, Korea and Egypt. By the time production of the F-4 slowed in the late 1970s, over 5,000 had been manufactured.

During the Vietnam War, the F-4 was the mount of legendary fighter leader and triple ace, Robin Olds. As commander of the 8th Tactical Fighter Wing, he was the mastermind behind Operation Bolo, a mission aimed at luring North Vietnamese MiGs into combat. On January 2, 1967, a force composed predominantly of F-4Cs approached the Hanoi area in a formation normally associated with a standard F-105 strike package. Cloud covered Hanoi and Olds had to trail his coat over the enemy airfields three times before MiG-21s began popping up on all sides. In the frenetic combat of the next few minutes, seven MiGs were shot down for no loss.

An extract from Colonel Olds' report of the action describes one success: "I fell in behind and below the MiG-21 at his seven o'clock position at about .95 Mach. Range was 4,500 ft, angle off 15. The MiG-21 obligingly pulled up well above the horizon and exactly down sun. I put the pipper on his tail pipe, received a perfect growl,

Above: Two red stars decorate the plate that prevents the turbulent boundary layer air from entering the left engine. The red stars on the plate belong to General Robin Olds and Lieutenant Stephen Crocker, who scored those aerial victories in this aircraft on May 20, 1967. In its air-to-ground role, the F-4 can carry twice the normal bomb load of a World War II B-17. Phantom II production ended in 1979 after more than 5,000 had been built — more than 2,600 for the USAF, about 1,200 for the Navy and Marine Corps, and the rest for friendly foreign nations. **Right:** The huge jet pipes of the F-4Cs General Electric J-79 engines. These powerful jets developed 17,000 pounds of thrust each, in afterburner, pushing the aircraft to speeds up to Mach 2.4 at altitude and Mach 1.2 lower down. The tail hook under the tail of the fighter is a hint of the aircraft's origins as a U.S. Navy carrier-borne fighter.

squeezed the trigger once, hesitated, then once again. The first Sidewinder leapt in front and within a split second turned left in a definite and beautiful collision course correction. The missile went slightly down, then arced gracefully up, heading for impact. Suddenly the MiG-21 erupted in a brilliant flash of orange flame. A complete wing separated and flew back in the airstream, together with a mass of smaller debris. The MiG swapped ends immediately, and tumbled forward for a few instants. It then fell, twisting, corkscrewing, tumbling, lazily toward the top of the clouds. No pilot ejection occurred."

Phantoms were equally successful as fighter-bombers and by 1972 they were carrying 2,000-pound Mk. 84 and 3,000-pound Mk. 118 bombs fitted with control surfaces and laser-seeking heads. Systematic attacks were made on the bridges of North Vietnam and the results were spectacular. On May 13, 16 F-4s delivered 24 "smart" bombs between them against the infamous Than Hoa bridge, wrecking a target that had defied U.S. airmen for years. (In attacks against the Than Hoa bridge on April 3, 1965, 638 750-pound bombs were dropped and 298 rockets fired, but it remained standing.) By the end of June, more than 400 bridges in North Vietnam had been destroyed or badly damaged. Phantoms were also formidable in the reconnaissance role, the RF-4C carrying multiple cameras, an infrared sensor, side-looking radar, and the TEREC electronic reconnaissance sensor.

By 1975, F-4G Phantoms became the USAF's "Wild Weasels" — aircraft modified to identify, locate and physically suppress or destroy ground-based enemy air defense systems. F-4Es had their cannon replaced with AN/APR-38 electronic warfare equipment and were rebuilt as F-4Gs, crewed by a pilot and an Electronic Warfare Officer. They carried the AGM-88A/B/C High-Speed Anti-Radiation Missile (HARM) and worked in tandem with other F-4G aircraft or as a hunter aircraft, directing fighter-bombers against SAM sites. In 1991, F-4G Wild Weasels were deployed in Operation Desert Storm. They flew 2,596 sorties and obliterated Iraqi air defenses in the opening stages of the war. Over 1,000 air-to-ground missiles were fired and more than 200 targets destroyed.

Brigadier General Robin Olds sits once again in the cockpit of his F-4 in the spring of 1997. As the CO of the 8th Tactical Fighter Wing, based at Ubon Royal Thai Air Force Base, flying F-4Cs, he planned a mission to lure MiGs carrying infrared homing devices into battle. He flew 107 combat missions in World War II and 152 combat missions in the Vietnam War. Robin Olds was enshrined into the National Aviation Hall of Fame in 2001.

B-52 Stratofortress

The Buff

IN 1954, STRATEGIC AIR COMMAND (SAC) began taking delivery of the aircraft that would come to symbolize U.S. strategic air power for generations of bomber aircrew — Boeing's B-52 Stratofortress, commonly known as the "Buff" (in genteel translation, Big Ugly Fat Fellow). In 1946, Boeing's design team had begun work on a very large bomber and they finally produced the immense B-52, powered by eight jet engines hung in four underwing pods. It was not long before SAC showed the world what the B-52 could do. In 1956, within a year of its arrival in the front line, a B-52 dropped a thermonuclear weapon with a yield of almost four megatons at Bikini Atoll. Global reach was demonstrated in January 1957 when three B-52s of the 93rd Bomb Wing, supported by KC-97 tankers, flew from California via Labrador, Morocco, Ceylon, the Philippines, Guam and Hawaii to complete a nonstop round-the-world flight of 24,325 miles in 45 hours and 19 minutes.

Originally intended to penetrate enemy defenses at high subsonic speeds and altitudes above 50,000 feet, the B-52 showed enormous capacity to absorb technological developments and adapt to changes in role and tactics. Its unrefueled radius of action of well over 4,000 miles became almost unlimited with flight refueling support. Over the years its maximum loaded weight rose to nearly half a million pounds as it took on more internal fuel, increased its weapon-carrying capacity, and accumulated various navigation and electronic defensive systems.

At the heart of the air-breathing element of the U.S. strategic deterrence triad during the Cold War, the B-52 also proved a force to be reckoned with in conventional warfare. During the

A B-52D rains bombs on North Vietnam. **Opposite:** The B-52 is the longest-serving combat aircraft ever, having been in front-line service since 1955. This B-52D is a dominating presence at the National Museum of the USAF.

Vietnam War, the firepower for tactical operations was vastly increased in June 1965 when SAC's B-52s were made available to fly combat missions. The B-52Fs that flew the first missions from Guam were modified to enable them to carry 27 750-pound bombs internally and 24 more on external racks. Later, B-52Ds went through a Big Belly modification allowing them to load the astonishing number of 84 500-pound bombs in the bay, while retaining the external capacity for 24 750-pound bombs. Although B-52 raids sometimes struck at empty forest, captured Viet Cong reported that they were the thing they most feared. With the bombers operating at 30,000 feet, nothing was seen or heard before hundreds of bombs arrived, obliterating everything over a huge area. For those who had survived the experience of a B-52 raid, wondering when the heavens would open again could concentrate the mind and weaken the spirit.

A little less than two years after they began, the 10,000th B-52 combat sortie was flown, and the big bombers were increasingly relied on to break up enemy troop concentrations. In 1968, the U.S. Marines' base at Khe Sanh was surrounded by 20,000 North Vietnamese regulars and remained under siege for 77 days. Operation Niagara, devised to provide the Marines with air support, included formations of three B-52s arriving over Khe Sanh every 90 minutes to bomb at the direction of the Combat Skyspot radar. Initially, a buffer zone allowed the B-52s to bomb no closer than 3,000 yards from the forward Marine positions. However, when enemy troops developed bunker complexes closer in, the Marine commander agreed to reduce the buffer to 1,000 feet. Ensuing strikes devastated enemy positions. A captured North

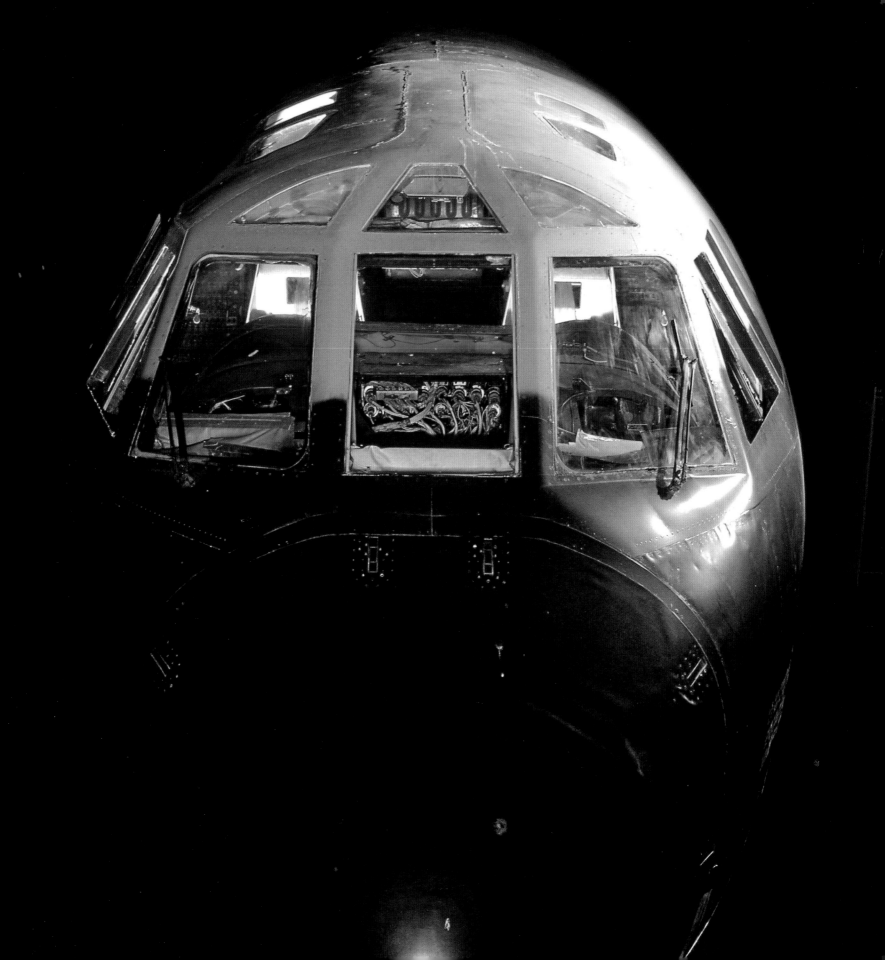

Vietnamese soldier estimated that one strike alone had killed 75 percent of an 1,800-man regiment.

In December 1972, as the Vietnam War moved into its closing stages, B-52s joined the Linebacker attacks on the North Vietnamese capital. After three days, the B-52 squadrons had flown 300 sorties but lost nine aircraft to the mass of SA-2s defending the city, six of which had been shot down on the third night. SAC therefore changed tactics. Raids were more concentrated in time, and B-52s bombed from varying heights and directions. Steep escape turns were avoided, because they produced large radar returns, and crews made random altitude changes to confuse the SAM operators. Using these tactics, only two more B-52s were lost on the four remaining nights up to Christmas Eve. The B-52s flew 729 sorties in 11 days and dropped over 15,000 tons of bombs. There can be little doubt that the Linebacker campaigns were instrumental in forcing the North Vietnamese back to the conference table. Peace talks were resumed on January 8 and the ceasefire document was signed on January 23, 1973.

B-52s were again involved during combat operations against Iraq and the Taliban in Afghanistan. In January 1991, B-52Gs opened Operation Desert Storm with a 35-hour mission from Barksdale AFB, Louisiana, the longest bombing raid ever at that time, launching cruise missiles at power stations and communications facilities in Iraq. Other B-52s flew from Diego Garcia in the Indian Ocean, and bases in the United Kingdom, Spain and Saudi Arabia were also used. The bombers were B-52Gs, carrying loads of 51 750-pound bombs to strike at targets like the Republican Guard troop concentrations. Flying in flights of three, they released 153 bombs at a time, carpeting an area one and a half miles long by a mile wide. The B-52 attacks shattered the morale of many Iraqi units, and were instrumental in persuading large numbers of soldiers to surrender as soon as the Coalition ground offensive was launched.

In one form or another, the B-52 has been operational since 1955. Over half a century later, the Buff has absorbed innumerable modifications and rebirths to remain a formidable aircraft. There is reason to believe that the aircraft's service life could extend to the year 2040, by which time it could be flown by the great-grandchildren of the original B-52 crews.

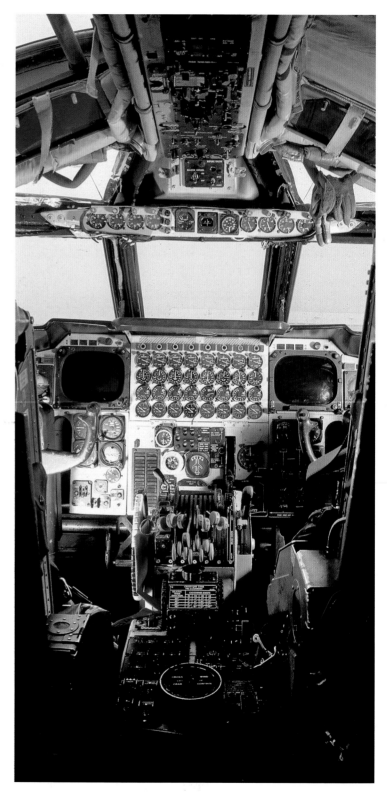

The updated cockpit of a B-52G. The control yokes and throttle quadrant will look familiar to original B-52 pilots, but the video screens and electronic sensors are evidence of how these warhorses have changed with the times and technologies of air war.

Above: The B-52D on display at the American Air Museum in England, at Duxford, is seen tail to tail with another Boeing bomber, the B-17. The B-52 was the last American bomber built with a tail-gun position. The B-17 had twin .50-caliber machine guns that were manually aimed. The B-52 had four and they were radar controlled.

Left: "Fitz" Fulton served in the USAF for 23 years in many roles including the Berlin Airlift and in Korea. He completed the Air Force Experimental Test Pilot School in 1952 and was assigned as the USAF pilot flying the B-52 for air-launching the X planes at Edwards AFB. He retired from the USAF in 1966 and joined NASA where, as their chief test pilot, he flew the XB-70 and the B-52 that launched the X-15.

Harrier

The Original Jump Jet

THE ROOTS OF THE HARRIER lie in the mid-1950s, a time when the possibility of vertical takeoff, fixed-wing aircraft was being investigated in several countries. Designers were stimulated by the growing military awareness of the vulnerability of large air bases to tactical nuclear weapons, and technological progress made such aircraft appear practicable. In Britain, Hawker Aircraft worked with the Bristol Engine Company (later Rolls-Royce) to develop the Pegasus-powered P.1127 and Kestrel experimental aircraft that led to the Harrier.

In 1970, the Harrier, the world's first operational V/STOL fighter, went into service with 4 Squadron in RAF Germany, introducing a new factor to the confrontation on NATO's Central Front. The Harrier's unique ability to be independent of fixed runways gave it an operational flexibility unattainable by more conventional warplanes. If war between NATO and the Warsaw Pact had broken out, Harriers could have been dispersed to pre-surveyed sites and housed in barns, bus stations, supermarkets, warehouses, or any other large buildings capable of rapid conversion to aircraft hangars. The equipment needed for logistics support of these sites was part of the Harrier package. Decried in its earliest form as an aircraft that could carry very little not very far, the Harrier was developed into a formidable weapons system. The RAF's night/all-weather Harrier II GR-7 version has provision for two 25 mm cannon, and is fitted with pylons capable of carrying 9,000 pounds of external stores, including a variety of bombs and rockets for close support, air-to-air missiles for intercept missions, reconnaissance pods, or nuclear weapons.

A Harrier GR7 of 20 (Reserve) Squadron, RAF Wittering, the unit responsible for training all RAF pilots joining front-line GR7 squadrons. **Opposite:** The Harrier GR3 on exhibit at the RAF Museum Hendon. The huge air intakes visible here are needed to feed the Rolls-Royce Pegasus 101 turbofan with four swivelling nozzles, developing 19,000 of thrust. The swiveling nozzles allow the versatile fighter to operate from very short fields and take off and land vertically without runways.

This development of the Harrier into a formidable fighting machine would not have been possible without the support of the U.S. Marine Corps. After USMC pilots flew the aircraft in 1968, orders were placed for a version designated AV-8A. Combining tactical mobility, responsiveness and basing flexibility, afloat and ashore, Harriers are well-suited to the combat requirements of the Marine Corps. The AV-8As were built in the United Kingdom, but arrangements were made with McDonnell Douglas for later licensed production in the United States. This guaranteed the aircraft's future, as the development of the AV-8B Harrier II for the Marines was led by the American company. A new and larger supercritical composite wing allowed the AV-8B to increase the number of stores pylons from four to seven, doubling the warload of its predecessor, and the new digital cockpit was state of the art, featuring HOTAS controls and a large HUD. New avionics included a stability augmentation system to make the machine easier to fly, and the Hughes Angle Rate Bombing System (ARBS) combining a laser spot tracker and TV imager working in concert to provide highly accurate targeting capabilities. Further improvements followed, giving the AV-8B a more advanced radar and a night attack capability.

During Operation Desert Storm in 1991, the Harrier II was the first Marine Corps tactical strike platform to arrive in theater. Three squadrons and one six-aircraft detachment operated ashore from an expeditionary airfield, while one squadron of 20 aircraft flew from amphibious shipping. During the ground war, AV-8Bs were the most forward deployed tactical strike aircraft in

During the Falklands conflict, Sea Harrier FRS 1s of the Fleet Air Arm's 801 Squadron shot down eight Argentine aircraft without loss.

theater, flying 3,380 sorties with a mission capable rate in excess of 90 percent.

In July 1980, the first ship of a new class was commissioned for the Royal Navy. Less than 20,000 tons loaded, the *Invincible* was at first known as a "through-deck-cruiser" and was intended to operate only helicopters, but a requirement was added to accommodate Sea Harriers. While two more ships of the *Invincible* class, *Illustrious* and *Ark Royal*, were being built, the Royal Navy refitted the old carrier *Hermes* for Sea Harrier operation. Prominent was a ski-jump ramp at the bow, added because Sea Harriers could get airborne from a small carrier deck with a heavier load if they used partial down nozzle and had an upward trajectory at lift-off. The modifications proved to have been inspired when, in 1982, the presence of *Hermes* and *Invincible* and their Sea Harriers enabled Britain to prevail in the Falklands War.

On paper, it seemed that the subsonic Sea Harriers must be outmatched in both numbers and performance by the Argentine Mirages/Daggers and A-4s. They were outnumbered by more than four to one, and the Mirages/Daggers were Mach 2 aircraft. However, the V/STOL Sea Harriers were capable of matching their speed to that of the ship and could fly in weather conditions too hazardous for conventional jet fighters. They also added the dimension of VIFFing (using Vectored thrust In Forward Flight). In combat, a Harrier pilot might choose to change the direction of his engine's thrust, either to bring the aircraft's nose up quickly to get off a shot, or to cause an opponent to overshoot during an attack by inducing rapid deceleration and an increased rate of turn. In addition, the Sea Harrier's AIM-9L Sidewinders were all-aspect missiles, and did not have to be fired from an enemy's rear quarter. There is little doubt that the British campaign could not have been conducted without the Sea Harrier/Sidewinder combination, which fought with great success, despite the small number of fighters engaged and the lack of an early warning system. Most notable was the Sea Harrier's record of 25 aircraft shot down without loss in aerial combat.

The Harrier's development into a potent multirole combat aircraft has spanned half a century, and has often been a difficult process. Nevertheless, the practicability and effectiveness of V/STOL operations has been established, and the Harrier experience has laid the foundation for future combat aircraft, notably the Lockheed-Martin J-35.

Left: The Harrier GR3. The Harrier owes its legacy to the original P1127, which hovered for the first time on October 21, 1960. P1127 was followed by the Kestrel, which, in turn, was followed by the first Harrier GR1.

Below: This is an RAF Harrier flying over England. The United States Marine Corps operates the AV-8 Harrier built by McDonnell-Douglas. The U.S. Marines employed these versatile fighters in Operation Desert Storm in 1991. During the ground war, AV-8Bs were based as close as 35 nautical miles (40.22 miles) from the Kuwait border, making them the most forward deployed tactical strike aircraft in theater.

Lockheed C-130

Hercules

THE C-130 HERCULES WAS inspired by the outbreak of the Korean War, and the realization that the USAF lacked a military transport capable of airlifting combat troops over medium distances and delivering them to rudimentary airfields. A requirement was issued by the USAF and the Lockheed proposal was rewarded with a contract. On August 23, 1954, the first of two YC-130A aircraft made its maiden flight, and the first production C-130A flew on April 7, 1955. Deliveries began in December 1956 and continued until the introduction of the C-130B in 1959. Several A-models, redesignated C-130D, were fitted with wheel/ski landing gear for service in the Arctic and for resupply missions to units along the Distant Early Warning (DEW) line. Six C-130Bs were modified in 1961 for midair recovery of USAF satellites, and a few, flown by Air National Guard units, were adapted for fire-fighting missions. The more powerful C-130E, which entered service in 1962, is an extended-range development of the C-130B. The maximum ramp weight of the E-model increased to 155,000 pounds, 20,000 pounds more than the B-model, and its fuel capacity was increased by over 17,000 pounds.

Troops and vehicles of the 1st Cavalry Division, U.S. Army with a C-130 Hercules of the 384th Air Division, in Vietnam.
Opposite: The C-130 continues to prove its worth, its rugged airframe and powerful engines still in service over 50 years after the prototype first flew. This C-130A at the National Museum of the USAF is the prototype gunship version of the Hercules, and saw action in Operation Desert Storm.

Hercules, designated KC-130 and equipped with removable fuel tanks in the cargo hold, perform invaluable service as tankers. Two wing-mounted hose and drogue refueling pods can each transfer up to 300 U.S. gallons per minute to two aircraft simultaneously, allowing for rapid cycle times of multiple-receiver aircraft formations. The C-130H is similar to the E-model, has more powerful turboprops, a redesigned outer wing, updated avionics, and other minor improvements. Delivery began in 1974

and the H-model remained in production until 1996. The newest version of the Hercules is the C-130J Super Hercules. It is the only model still produced and is very different from its predecessors. The differences include Rolls-Royce Allison AE2100 turboprops with composite six-bladed scimitar propellers, digital avionics with head-up displays for each pilot, increased reliability and up to 27 percent lower operating costs. The C-130J is also available in a standard-length or stretched C-130J-30 version. Lockheed received the launch order for the J model from the RAF, who ordered 25 aircraft, with deliveries beginning in 1999.

During the Vietnam War, the C-130 was the most important theater transport for bulk movement, registering a high figure of 69,499 tons transported in one month, and, in the 77-day siege of Khe Sanh in 1968, 92 percent of all supplies were flown in by C-130s. The ubiquitous Hercules was also involved in many other missions. Some USAF C-130As were converted into gunships. In addition to their side-firing 20 mm Vulcan cannons and 7.62 mm miniguns, they also possessed sensors, a target acquisition system, and a forward-looking infrared (FLIR) and low-light television system. Other C-130 roles included acting as aerial command posts, starting forest fires by dropping oil drums, sowing anti-personnel mines during the interdiction of the Ho Chi Minh Trail in Laos, and clearing instant helicopter landing zones in the forest with huge weapons such as the 15,000-pound BLU-82 bomb. Ryan RPV reconnaissance drones were launched from C-130s and, although programmed for particular profiles, their progress could be

Above: *Coronet Oak,* by Gil Cohen. During Operation Coronet Oak, members of the 179th Airlift Wing, West Virginia, and the 130th Airlift Wing, Ohio, prepare for their missions while a C-130 from Rhode Island's 143rd Airlift Wing takes off from Howard Air Force Base, Panama.
Opposite: In the shadow of the broad wings are the twin 40 mm Bofors guns; further forward are the pair of six-barrel 20 mm cannons.

adjusted by the controller in the C-130 as necessary. By 1969, the commander of a rescue mission was usually flying in an HC-130P, which was equipped as a tanker and carried a tracker system for locating downed airmen. C-130s were prominent during the final withdrawal from Vietnam, airlifting Americans and South Vietnamese refugees out of Tan Son Nhut airport, Saigon. Load restrictions were removed on April 20, 1975, and the transports began setting records, with C-130s taking as many as 260 people when the normal limit was 75.

Some 150 Hercules were deployed in support of Operations Desert Shield and Desert Storm. These aircraft moved units to forward bases once they arrived in the theatre. From August 10, 1990, to the ceasefire, Air Force C-130s flew 46,500 sorties and moved more than 209,000 people and 300,000 tons of supplies within the theater. They provided logistical support, aeromedical evacuation of the wounded, and battlefield mobility. During the "100-hour" ground campaign, C-130s flew more than 500 sorties a day. With their computerized frequency scanning ability and batteries of jammers, EC-130H Compass Call aircraft swamped the Iraqi airwaves, rendering reliable radio communication almost impossible for the enemy. First cousins to the EC-130H are the EC-130E PsyWar aircraft flown by the Pennsylvania Air National Guard.

C-130s have been involved in some unusual operations in their long history. In 1976, Israeli commandos carried out a surprise assault at Entebbe Airport, Uganda, to rescue 103 passengers of an airliner hijacked by terrorists. The rescue force (200 soldiers, jeeps, and a black Mercedes-Benz resembling Ugandan dictator Idi Amin's vehicle of state) was flown 2,500 miles from Israel to Entebbe by five Israeli Air Force (IAF) Hercules aircraft. The Hercules also holds the record for the largest and heaviest aircraft to land on an aircraft carrier. In November 1963, a C-130 landed on the USS *Forrestal* without using the ship's arrester gear. The test was successful, but the idea was considered too risky for routine Carrier Onboard Delivery operations.

In the five decades since the USAF issued its specification, the astonishing C-130 Hercules has become an invaluable multirole aircraft and has remained in continuous production. Besides its varied military roles, it has fought fires, tracked icebergs, flown in hurricanes, carried Muslims to Mecca, taken Ethiopian Jews to Israel, and hauled a live whale and the occasional camel. There are more than 40 versions of the Hercules and it is widely used by at least 60 nations. The C-130 has the longest continuous production run of any military aircraft in history. It is arguably the most successful military transport ever built, and it will continue in production well into the 21st century.

F-15 Eagle

Big Bird

THE APPEARANCE OF THE outstanding Soviet MiG-23 and MiG-25 fighters in the late 1960s encouraged the American development of more advanced aircraft. In reviewing its combat power, the USAF had to take account of the need both to deter (and, if necessary, fight) the USSR and to retain a capability to intervene in small wars affecting U.S. interests wherever they might occur. Here the lessons of Vietnam were invaluable. When the F-4 first appeared in Southeast Asia, it was fast, but it was also large, not very agile, gunless, and trailed the signature of smoking engines. A strap-on cannon and the addition of leading edge slats helped a bit, but something better was needed. (Besides, it was time the Air Force had really capable fighters that had not been designed for the Navy!)

The perfect answer came in the shape of the McDonnell Douglas F-15 Eagle, an aircraft able to make the most of the electronics revolution of the 1970s and designed from the outset as an air superiority fighter. The F-15 first flew in 1972 and reached front-line squadrons in 1975. Even larger than the F-4, the F-15 is immensely powerful, its two 24,000-pound-thrust Pratt & Whitney turbofans giving a clean aircraft a thrust-to-weight ratio of better than one at sea level. Its astonishing agility is born of this great power and the generous area of its delta shaped wing. Pilots revel in the all-round visibility from the high bubble canopy, and in the systems that simplify the business of flying and fighting the Eagle — notably the head-up display and the HOTAS (Hands On Throttle And Stick) arrangement of essential switches. The F-15's size allows space for the most comprehensive avionics and weapons control systems, and for an integral Vulcan cannon plus a wide variety of external stores.

F-15 Eagles of 133 Squadron, Israeli Air Force, in formation.
Opposite: On display at the National Museum of the USAF, this F-15A, 76-027, was delivered to the 27th Tactical Fighter Squadron, 1st Tactical Fighter Wing, at Langley Air Force Base, Virginia, and is painted in the colors of that squadron.

It also made the Eagle an obvious candidate for development as a long-range, all-weather interdiction aircraft — the two-seat F-15E, capable of carrying 24,500 pounds of ordnance.

Designed in the 1960s and built in the 1970s, the F-15A–D series have been in service for well over a quarter of a century. While the Eagle's aerodynamics and maneuverability has remained impressive, quantum leaps in integrated circuit technology in the 1990s made the original F-15 avionics suite obsolete. The Multi-Stage Improvement Program (MSIP) was designed to allow the F-15 to maintain air superiority in a dense hostile environment into the late 1990s and beyond. A new central computer with much faster processing speed and greater memory capacity upgraded the F-15 to 1990s technology, adding capacity needed to support improved radar and other systems. Upgraded F-15s entered the 21st century fitted with JTIDS (Joint Tactical Information Distribution System), PACS (Programmable Armament Control Set), MPCD (Multi-Purpose Color Display) for expanded weapons control, monitoring, and release capabilities featured a modern touch screen that allowed the pilot to talk to his weapons, DTM (Data Transfer Module) to allow a planned route to be flown using mission planning computers, and an improved ICS (internal countermeasures set) to detect threats and provide a self-protection radar jamming capability that allowed pilots to react to threat and to maneuver to break the lock of enemy missiles.

As of 2005, the F-15 in all air forces had achieved a kill record of 104 kills to 0 losses in air combat (excluding a Japanese F-15J shot down by its partner in 1995 due to an AIM-9 Sidewinder

safety malfunction during air-to-air combat training). Over half the F-15's kills were claimed by Israeli Air Force pilots. During Israeli-Lebanese border disputes in 1979/81, F-15As shot down 13 Syrian MiG-21s and two Syrian MiG-25s. In the 1982 Lebanon War, the Israeli F-15s destroyed 40 Syrian jet fighters (23 MiG-21s and seventeen MiG-23s) and one SA.342L Gazelle helicopter. In 1985, during Syrian/Israeli skirmishes, Israel reported the downing of two Syrian MiG-23s by F-15s. Royal Saudi Air Force F-15C pilots shot down two F-4Es flown by the Iranian Air Force in a border skirmish in 1984, and two Iraqi Mirage F1s during the 1991 Gulf War. USAF F-15C pilots had 34 confirmed kills of Iraqi aircraft during the Gulf War, mostly by missile fire: two MiG-29s, two MiG-25s, eight MiG-23s, two MiG-21s, two Su-25s, four Su-22s, one Su-7, six Mirage F1s, one Il-76, one Pilatus PC-9 trainer, and two Mi-8 helicopters. After air superiority was achieved in the first three days of the conflict, many of the later kills were reportedly of Iraqi aircraft fleeing to Iran. The single-seat F-15C was used for air superiority, and the F-15E was heavily used in air-to-ground attacks. An F-15E achieved an aerial kill of another Iraqi Mi-8 helicopter using a laser-guided bomb during the air war. F-15Es sustained two losses to ground fire in 1991. USAF F-15C's also shot down four Yugoslav MiG-29s during Operation Allied Force, NATO's 1999 intervention in Kosovo. Not all F-15 victories were well welcomed by the USAF. In 1994, two U.S. Army UH-60 Black Hawk's were misidentified before being fired on in error and shot down by F15Cs in the Northern nofly zone of Iraq.

The almost clinically impersonal nature of late-20th-century air warfare was summarized by one victorious F-15C pilot, Capt Charles Magill, a Marine exchange officer flying with the 33rd Tactical Fighter Wing: "When you get down to the bottom line, everything was incredibly basic. Weapons system set up just right, shoot your ordnance at the first opportune moment, watch the MiG blow up, and get the hell out."

During a "Red Flag" exercise at Nellis AFB, an F-15 thunders off the runway. Red Flag is a mission readiness exercise that simulates the realities of an air war.

Above: On the ramp at Nellis AFB, these F-15E "Strike Eagle" aircraft are being prepared for a Red Flag mission. **Right:** An F-15E from the 57th Fighter Wing, based at Nellis AFB, taxis to the runway. The mission of the 57th Wing is to provide advanced aerospace training to worldwide combat air forces and showcase aerospace power to the world. The Wing oversees the dynamic and challenging missions for all flying operations at Nellis AFB, including USAF Weapons School, "Red Flag," "Air Warrior" training and the Air Warfare Center's test and evaluation activities.

Boeing Jet Airliners

World Shrinkers

IN THE POST-WWII WORLD, no name became more closely associated with the explosive growth of air travel than that of Boeing. At first, Boeing's dominance seemed anything but assured. The company entered the postwar civil aviation field with the piston-engined Stratocruiser. When it first flew in July 1947, the Stratocruiser could fly higher, faster and further than its competitors, but it was costly both to operate and to buy and it was not an economic success.

Unable to make inroads into the civil airliner market, Boeing was kept alive by military sales. These included the B-47, a revolutionary jet bomber with swept wings and podded engines. The experience gained with the B-47 proved invaluable in laying the foundations for commercial success. Boeing's executives decided that if the company were to have a future in the commercial field it would have to be based on a jet transport with transatlantic range. With an eye on a possible military requirement, the new Boeing was given the model number 367-80. This misleading designation suggested that it was the 80th design study based on the Model 367, the USAF's KC-97. Forever after, the prototype was known as the Dash 80. However, Boeing could not attract advance orders for an aircraft developed from the Dash 80. Undeterred, the company went ahead with construction of the prototype, gambling $16 million that jet transports would prove to be both efficient and reliable.

Boeing's gamble paid off in October 1955 when Pan American ordered twenty 707s. By 1956, there had been a flood of orders for two jet airliners, the Boeing 707 and the later Douglas DC-8, but in terms of numbers Boeing gained the upper hand. It was a decisive advantage that would never be relinquished. Once established, the

A Boeing 377 Stratocruiser, Pan American's Clipper *Morning Star,* flies past the Cunard Line's *Queen Elizabeth.* The advent of intercontinental airline traffic, beginning in the mid-1950s, destroyed the transatlantic ocean liner trade. **Opposite:** The Boeing Jumbo jet — the 747 — represents the airline business as a whole in its capacity, reliability and adaptability. This 747 began its career flying passengers and now has been converted to hauling packages for United Parcel Service.

707 ($5 million) showed that one airliner could carry as many transatlantic passengers each year as the *Queen Mary* ocean liner ($30 million) while incurring about one-tenth the fuel costs.

By 1960, Boeing was pressing ahead with a "mini 707" design featuring a cluster of three engines at the rear. The Boeing 727 was designed to meet competing requirements from Eastern and United Airlines. Eastern wanted an aircraft able to operate from La Guardia's 4,860-foot runway, and United needed an airliner that could reach either U.S. coast with a full load after taking off "hot and high" from Denver. Boeing's new wing took care of the problem with leading edge flaps and slats, together with triple slotted trailing edge flaps. To passengers, the disassembling of the wing on final approach could look disturbing, the ground below appearing through gaps where a solid wing had been only moments before, leaving the 727 apparently reliant on levitation rather than lift. The 727 attracted orders worldwide and when production ceased in 1984, it was the most successful jet airliner to that date, 1,832 having been built.

The Boeing 737 appeared in 1967. Smaller than the 727, it offered commonality with other Boeing airliners and six abreast seating. Unflatteringly nicknamed "Fat Albert," the 737 was "all square" — about 100 feet long, 100 feet across, and intended for around 100 passengers. By the end of the century, variants had been built to carry up to 200 passengers, haul freight, fulfill a number of military roles, and satisfy the demands of lofty executives for luxury travel. Three generations of 737s had been redesigned to accommodate new engines and avionics. "Fat Albert" had become the phenomenon of the jet age, with almost 4,000 aircraft being

flown by some 330 civil operators and the military of a dozen countries. As the 21st century dawned, 737s had carried some 6 billion people — the equivalent of the world population.

Developments in the aviation world during the 1960s — big turbofans, new construction materials and methods, better airports, increasing demand for air travel — all suggested that the airlines were ready to take the next step. Boeing's Model 747 was rolled out on September 30, 1968. When its six million parts came together, the 747 was probably the most complex single machine ever built. The gigantic aircraft was to be capable of accommodating up to 550 passengers at costs per passenger/mile that were some 30 percent less than the 707. Teething troubles with any new type are inevitable, and the 747 was no exception, but not all were faults with the aircraft. The 747's great size and enormous weight affected ground equipment, taxiways, parking slots, ticketing, catering and baggage handling. During the first two years of operation, the problems of how to cope with the 747 were gradually worked out and its popularity with passengers grew. The 747 became the flagship for airlines worldwide, making intercontinental travel a possibility for more and more people. By the end of the century, Boeing's "Jumbo" had carried over two billion passengers, flown 50 million hours and covered some 20 billion air miles.

As the 707 and 727 fleets aged, Boeing produced two twin-turbofan airliners — the narrow-bodied, single-aisle 757 (230 seats) and the wide-bodied double-aisle 767 (289 seats). Both aircraft proved to be some 30 percent more economical than their predecessors

and were immediately successful. Even so, Boeing found that its traditional customers were looking for a third aircraft, bigger than the 767 but smaller than the 747. The Boeing 777 first flew on June 12, 1994. A wide-bodied twin with a maximum of 440 seats, the 777 weighed over 500,000 pounds at takeoff and was powered by two turbofans of some 80,000 pounds thrust each. By the late 1990s, the stretched 777-300 version was capable of carrying up to 400 passengers and flying them from New York to Tokyo in fourteen hours at seat/mile costs 30 percent lower than the 747.

For the 21st century, Boeing began developing the 787 Dreamliner, designed for super-efficiency and intended to "provide new solutions for airlines and passengers." Two Dreamliner models, the 787-8 and 787-9, will carry 223 to 259 passengers in tri-class configurations on routes up to 8,500 nautical miles. A third variant, the 787-3, will accommodate 296 passengers in two classes over routes of 3,500 nautical miles. By jet airliner standards, the new aircraft is mid-size, but is planned to provide airlines with long-range capability through unmatched fuel efficiency. The 787's advances will be possible because most of the primary structure, including the fuselage and wing, will be made of composite materials. The aircraft will also incorporate "health-monitoring systems that will allow the airplane to self-monitor and report maintenance requirements to ground-based computer systems." Launch of the 787 program occurred in April 2004 with an order from All-Nippon Airways. Production of the 787 will begin in 2006. First flight is expected in 2007 with certification, delivery and entry into service occurring in 2008.

Boeing's 757 and 767 were developed in tandem and entered service within five months of each other. The 757 has a standard single-aisle configuration in the passenger cabin. The 767 has a larger, two-aisle cabin.

Top: Perhaps the most famous Boeing 707 is USAF 26000, known as *Air Force One* when the American President was on board. It is seen here the day it was retired to the National Museum of the USAF on May 20, 1998. **Above Left:** Alvin "Tex" Johnston, one of America's foremost test pilots and winner of the Thompson Trophy in 1946 at the National Air Races. He joined Boeing in 1948 as senior test pilot on the XB-47 Stratojet and as project pilot for the YB-52. He had such confidence in the prototype of the 707, called the Dash 80, that he barrel-rolled the airliner several times during a demonstration flight. **Above Right:** The Boeing Type 367-80 (Dash 80) was rolled out of the Renton hangar near Seattle on May 14, 1954.

Rutan's Originals

Shapes for the Future

ELBERT LEANDER "BURT" RUTAN is an aerospace engineer noted for his flair for designing unconventional aircraft. As a schoolboy, he designed and built award-winning model aircraft, and he was sixteen when he flew solo in an Aeronca Champ. In 1965 he graduated from California Polytechnic University with an aeronautical engineering degree, and in June of 1974 he formed the Rutan Aircraft Factory (RAF) to develop light homebuilt aircraft. The first aircraft produced at the RAF was the two-seat wood-and-fiberglass VariViggen, a pusher canard that Rutan started to design as an undergraduate in the early 1960s. It was the forerunner to a series of Rutan general aviation and homebuilt aircraft that made use of composite materials and differed dramatically from the more conventional designs produced elsewhere in the aviation industry. Among them were the VariEze, Quickie, Defiant, Long-EZ, Grizzly and Catbird. Other designs included the NASA AD-1, a small jet aircraft built to demonstrate a wing that could pivot during flight; the Solitaire, a canard sailplane; and the Amsoil Racer, a staggered-wing biplane that competed in the Reno air races.

SpaceShipOne flies under the wide wings of Scaled Composites' mother ship *White Knight,* on its way to permanent display in the Milestones of Flight Gallery at the National Air and Space Museum. *SpaceShipOne* was the first privately developed aircraft to reach space. **Opposite:** *Voyager*, by Paul Rendel. Buffeted by storms during the nonstop round-the-world flight, *Voyager's* long wings bend and flex in turbulent air.

Burt Rutan formed Scaled Composites in 1982. Efficiency, low-cost manufacturing techniques, and energy conservation were the primary goals. In the early 1980s, Beechcraft produced Rutan's Starship, a typically futuristic variable-sweep canard design employing an all-graphite composite airframe and with yaw control provided by wing-tip fins rather than a conventional rudder. Once again, Rutan used a pusher configuration, pushing instead of pulling the aircraft along. This offered a quieter ride, placing the twin turboprops aft of the eight-passenger cabin. Aluminum mesh embedded into the skin shielded the Starship's electronics from lighting strikes, permitting electric current to flow through the body to a point where the charge exited the aircraft. Beech's $350-million investment resulted in a high-performance, stall-free aircraft, and the Starship was certified by the FAA in June 1988. Nevertheless, despite the exotic appeal of the concept and the innovative genius of the design, only 53 Starships were ever built. By the time the aircraft was for sale in 1989, the list price was $3.9 million, similar to the Cessna Citation V and Lear 31 jets, which could cruise some 100 knots faster than the Starship.

Burt Rutan is perhaps most famous for his design of record-breaking aircraft, including the *Voyager* and the *Global Flyer*. It seemed almost inconceivable that an aircraft could be built with the range to fly unrefueled round the world, but that is what Rutan set out to do. The result was the *Voyager*, an unconventional two-place, twin-engined aircraft made of lightweight composite material, mainly a sandwich of honeycomb paper and graphite fiber, which kept the structural weight under 1,000 pounds. At takeoff, however, *Voyager* weighed well over 9,000 pounds. Most of that was fuel, more than 7,000 pounds of it in 17 tanks. The lift was provided by 110-foot-span high-aspect-ratio wings so flexible that the tips deflected upward some 5 feet in flight. Power came from two Teledyne Continental engines mounted in tandem, the one in front producing 130 horsepower and the one behind 110 horsepower. Both engines were used together only for takeoff or for emergency maneuvering. In flight, the *Voyager* cruised on the rear engine alone. Efficient use of power was essential, since the aircraft had to average 4 miles per pound of fuel (24 miles to the U.S. gallon).

Above: *SpaceShipOne* nestled under the cockpit of the mother ship. The dark panel under the nose of the spacecraft is for thermal protection during ascent and when reentering the atmosphere. **Right:** Scaled Composites test pilot Mike Melvill, speaking at the Wright Memorial near Dayton, Ohio. Mike Melvill is vice president and general manager of Scaled Composites; he has 24 years of experience as a test pilot, and has logged nearly 7,000 hours in over 130 types of aircraft. In 1999, he received the Iven C. Kincheloe trophy from the Society of Experimental Test Pilots for his work in development testing Scaled Composites Model 281 Proteus, a tandem-wing high-endurance aircraft designed by Burt Rutan to investigate the use of aircraft as high-altitude telecommunications relays. On the morning of June 21, 2004, Melvill was the pilot for *SpaceShipOne*'s first spaceflight and the first privately funded human spaceflight mission to reach space. In a ceremony two hours after landing, was awarded his astronaut wings, specifically the FAA Commercial Astronaut badge, the first wings awarded for a non-government space program and the first for a space plane flight since the X-15 flights of the 1960s.

The pilots chosen were Dick Rutan and Jeana Yeager. In taking on the flight, they knew that they would be sharing a compartment just seven and a half feet long and three and a half feet across for more than a week. They took off on December 14, 1986, from Edwards Air Force Base, California, using 14,200 feet of runway to get airborne. From then on the principal challenge for Rutan and Yeager was to cope with the physical and mental strain of being confined for days on end in a coffin-sized space while flying in long straight lines and listening to the unchanging note of the rear engine. *Voyager* landed back at Edwards AFB just over nine days after taking off. It had been a close run thing. Almost 99 percent of their fuel load was gone. The official distance flown was 24,986 statute miles at an average speed of 115.65 miles per hour. Almost as an afterthought it was observed that, for the first time, the world records for distance in a straight line and over a closed circuit had been set at the same time.

On March 3, 2005, the Virgin Atlantic *Global Flyer*, another Rutan aircraft similar to the *Voyager* but built of stiffer materials and powered by a jet engine, completed the first solo nonstop, non-refueled flight around the world with Steve Fossett as the pilot. In February 2006, Fossett did it again over a longer route in 76 hours, 45 minutes, the *Global Flyer* in the process setting the absolute record for the longest flight ever made by any aircraft — 26,389 statute miles.

Burt Rutan's creative genius has also reached into space. On June 21, 2004, *SpaceShipOne*, piloted by Mike Melvill, became the first private manned craft to leave the Earth's atmosphere. In October of that year, *SpaceShipOne* exceeded an altitude of 328,000 feet twice within 14 days, thus claiming the $10-million Ansari X-Prize. Pilot Brian Binnie also broke Joe Walker's unofficial world altitude record of 354,200 feet, achieved in the X-15, by rocketing to 367,442 feet above the Earth's surface. Building on this success, Rutan is designing two more spacecraft. *Spaceship 2*, being produced for Richard Branson's Virgin Galactic, is intended to begin space tourism flights in 2008, and *Spaceship 3* is being developed to carry passengers to the International Space Station.

During his illustrious career, Burt Rutan's creativity and ingenuity have earned him almost every honor the aviation world can bestow. His innovative designs and extensive use of composite materials have redefined the way aircraft can be designed and built. Throughout his remarkable career, his work has been marked by flair and enthusiasm. As he says: "I'm doing essentially the same kind of thing I did when I was as a kid except I'm doing it with rocket ships and airplanes and special vehicles."

Looking like a craft from another solar system, but only from Mojave, California, the mated aircraft silhouetted in a hangar at Wright-Patterson AFB. The *White Knight* carries the *SpaceShip* to high altitude and then releases the smaller aircraft/spaceship for its flight into space. This is a time-tested method of launching rocket planes; the X-15 also featured in this book, at page 154, was air-launched from a B-52.

Lockheed F-117A

Stealthy Nighthawk

ALMOST UNNOTICED, AN EXTRAORDINARY aircraft made its operational debut in December 1989 during Operation Just Cause, the U.S. intervention in Panama. Rio Hato airfield was attacked by a pair of Lockheed F-117A Nighthawks. Their efforts were not particularly noteworthy, but the mission served as a muted prelude. The complete Nighthawk work with full fortissimo orchestration followed two years later in the Middle East.

Lockheed Advanced Development Projects (the "Skunk Works") was awarded a contract in 1978 for the development and production of F-117As. The first flight followed only 31 months later, and deliveries began in August 1982. Operational capability was achieved by the 4450th Tactical Group, (later the 37th and then 49th Tactical Fighter Wing) in October 1983, and production ended in the summer of 1990, after 59 Nighthawks had been delivered to the USAF. Existence of the aircraft was denied until 1988, and it was not until April 1990 that an example was seen in public.

The F-117A is constructed mainly of aluminum alloy, with some titanium in the engine and exhaust systems. The outer skin is covered by radar absorption material and every facet of the aircraft's surface is angled at least 30 degrees from the vertical to reflect radar beams away from radars. There are sawtooth edges on the intersection of cockpit and fuselage, and on access panels and bomb bay doors. Other stealth design features include engine inlet grills on either side of the forward fuselage shielding engine compressor blades from detection by radar. At the aft end, thin engine exhaust slots minimize the aircraft's infrared signature by dissipating the plume

Low observable technology, better known as Stealth, evidenced here in the F-117. This is the world's first aircraft designed using stealth technology. **Opposite:** The many facets of the arrowhead-shaped F-117 Nighthawk. The fighter is manufactured from radar absorbent materials. The canopy opening of the fighter shows some of the secrets of low observable design. The sawtooth pattern along the bottom edge breaks up the incoming radar signals and sends them off into diverse directions, making the fighter less visible to the searching electronic eyes.

from the two General Electric F404 turbofans. The airframe behind the exhaust slots is covered with heat-reflecting tiles, and bypass air from the engines is used to cool down the rear of the aircraft. A typical fighter has a head-on radar cross-section of about 5 square meters. The F-117A has an effective radar cross section of 0.01 square meters or less.

The Nighthawk is inherently unstable about all three axes, but its quadruple-redundant fly-by-wire controls and state-of-the-art digital avionics suite, together with an automated mission planning system, make it relatively easy to fly. The computerized systems make constant adjustments to the F-117A's control surfaces and maintain stability. Four elevons give control in roll and pitch. Directional control is provided by a pair of all-flying tails arranged in a V. The hinge line on the moveable tail is Z-shaped, in accord with the stealth principle of avoiding straight edges, and the all-flying rudders are faceted to reduce radar reflectivity.

The F-117A's internal weapons bay can carry 5,000 pounds of ordnance. It can accept two examples of nearly any weapon in the USAF inventory, including the B61 nuclear bomb, but typical loads are a pair of GBU-10, GBU-12 or GBU-27 laser-guided bombs, two BLU-109 penetration bombs, two Wind-Corrected Munition Dispensers (WCMD), two Joint Direct Attack Munitions (JDAMs), or a GPS/INS guided stand-off bomb. The F-117A relies on its ability to remain undetected and so has no weapons for self-protection. Detailed planning for missions into highly defended target areas is accomplished by an automated mission planning system developed specifically to take advantage of the F-117A's unique capabilities.

After their minor supporting role in Panama in 1989, Nighthawks surreptitiously led the air assault in the first Gulf War just over a year later. They began Operation Desert Storm by attacking radars close to Baghdad and then a communications center in the city. Before the night was out, the Nighthawks had hit 34 targets, using a variety of laser-guided bombs. Command centers, control bunkers, critical bridges and the like were almost invariably struck with startling accuracy. Only 36 Nighthawks were deployed in Desert Storm, but they flew more than a third of the bombing runs on the first day of the war. During the six weeks of Desert Storm, Nighthawks completed more than 1,250 sorties, dropped some 2,000 tons of bombs, and flew over 6,900 hours. More than 3,000 antiaircraft guns and 60 surface-to-air missile batteries protected Baghdad, but the Nighthawks operated in Iraqi airspace at night with impunity.

F-117As were similarly active in Kosovo during 1999, when one F-117 was lost to Serbian forces. On March 27, 1999, F-117A serial number 82-806 was shot down by a Neva-M missile (NATO designation SA-3 "Goa"). Several SA-3s were launched, one of which detonated close to the F-117A, forcing the pilot to eject. Parts of the aircraft are now exhibited in the Museum of Yugoslav Aviation in Belgrade. Two other F-117As were lost in accidents when flying from their base in Nevada during the 1980s.

Nighthawks were active once again during the 2003 invasion of Iraq. The assault on Iraq began in the early hours (local time) of March 20, 2003. That morning, intelligence suggested that Saddam and his sons, Qusay and Uday, were with other Baathist leaders in a specific building in Baghdad. Two F-117As were scrambled from Kuwait and, just before dawn, four 2,000-pound "bunker-busting" EGBU-27 bombs hit the target, but it was too late. The birds had flown, but Saddam was left in no doubt that he was a hunted man, liable to attract a direct and devastating attack if any one of his entourage ever dared to betray his whereabouts. The F-117A attack illustrated several characteristics of 21st-century aerial warfare. Aircraft were on their way less than two hours after the crews received their orders. The attackers were "stealthy" and the bombs were "smart." In all their operations against Saddam Hussein's forces, F-117As continued to demonstrate their remarkable capabilities. However, there was no escaping the fact that they had been designed in the late 1970s. Their stealth technology, while still more advanced than that of any other aircraft but the B-2 and F-22A, is expensive and difficult to maintain. The facet-based stealth design (with its aerodynamic cost) represents a technique that has since been greatly refined. Successful though it has been, the brilliantly conceived Nighthawk has been in the USAF's front-line for a quarter of a century and is nearing the end of its combat life. Its distinctive shape will no longer be seen in the skies after 2008.

GBU-12 Paveway II 500-pound bombs were used by F-117As during Operation Desert Storm. These weapons are carried internally and only exposed when an attack is made, thus maintaining the low observable profile of the aircraft and allowing it to operate in Iraqi airspace at night with impunity.

Crouching in its hangar, an F-117A Nighthawk. This photo from Lockheed's photo staff shows off the unusual shapes and designs of this first operational "stealth" fighter. The non-traditional shape of the aircraft and a designed instability makes the computer-managed flight-control systems essential for it to fill the role of a reliable military fighter-bomber.

Jack Northrop's Dream

The B-2 Spirit

JACK NORTHROP WAS A VISIONARY as an aircraft designer. He began examining the idea of a flying wing in the 1920s, believing that this was the way to higher performance and greater aerodynamic efficiency. He was sure that such a design, without a conventional fuselage and tail assembly, would produce much less drag as it moved through the air. This would result in significant advantages, such as higher speed, or the ability to carry heavier loads over greater ranges. Northrop built his first crude flying wing aircraft then, but it proved difficult to control. Not until 1940, by which time he had the money and the resources needed to allow him to pursue his ideas again, was he able to begin work on his N-1M, the first true flying wing. Extensive wind-tunnel tests were carried out with flying wing models, and the design incorporated airfoil sections with low drag and improved stability, besides using various high-lift devices, spoilers, and flaps. The N1-M showed that an all-wing design could fly successfully, and the work done on that aircraft eventually led to a proposal for a bomber, the XB-35.

In January 1941, the U.S. Army began to consider developing bombers with intercontinental range. Northrop was contacted in May 1941 and asked to provide studies of a flying wing proposal with a range of 8,000 miles at 25,000 feet while carrying a ton of bombs at a cruising speed of 250 miles per hour. Four one-third-scale N9M test aircraft were built, but development did not go smoothly and the program fell behind schedule. The first full-size bomber, the XB-35, did not fly until June 25, 1946, and then there were serious problems with the four piston engines and their propellers. Northrop modified the design to accept eight jet

Low observable aviation technology made large: the B-2. This heavy stealth bomber has a range of more than 6,000 miles unrefueled and over 10,000 nautical miles with one refueling, giving it the ability to fly to any place in the world within hours. **Opposite:** Jack Northrop believed that a flying wing would be efficient. It took nearly 40 years of technology to create the flight control systems that could keep the naturally unstable design in the air.

engines, and the aircraft was redesignated YB-49, but more problems arose. The J35 turbojets were extremely thirsty, and the YB-49 had only half the range of its piston-engined predecessor. The test pilots reported that it was difficult to hold a steady course or a constant airspeed and altitude, and that there was a persistent yawing motion. Disaster struck on June 5, 1948, when a YB-49 crashed just north of Muroc Dry Lake, killing the pilot, Captain Glenn Edwards, and his crew of four. (Muroc AFB was renamed in honor of Glenn Edwards.) It was becoming clear that the technology available in the late 1940s was inadequate for overcoming many of the problems associated with flying wings and, on March 15, 1950, the YB-49 program was canceled.

Jack Northrop died in 1981, so did not live to see his faith in the flying wing justified. His concept remained dormant until the appearance of the B-2 Spirit stealth bomber nearly forty years after the last flight of the YB-49. The B-2 appeared in November 1988, offering a dramatic contrast with the more conventional USAF heavy bombers, the B-1B and the B-52. Its smooth lines gave promise that it would knife through the air, making the most of an excellent lift/drag ratio to carry heavy loads over long distances. The new bomber's shape was both efficient and inherently stealthy, and quadruple-redundant fly-by-wire flight controls were married to a sophisticated air-data system, eliminating the stability and control problems that had plagued YB-49. Flight controls located on the wing's trailing edge performed the functions of ailerons, elevators and rudders on conventional aircraft. A "beaver tail" flap provided trim for the pitch axis and helped to offset the effects of turbu-

Ninety years to the day that the Wrights first flew their 1903 Flyer, on December 17, 1993, the first B-2 was delivered to the USAF. Its very slim profile makes it almost disappear against the ever-changing sky.

lence. Test pilots reported that the handling qualities of the B-2 were outstanding — it looked good and it flew well. "You put the nose right where you want it, and it stays there — there's no hunting or oscillating...you don't have to fight with this plane." Development proceeded without undue difficulty and the first aircraft, named *Spirit of Missouri,* was delivered to the USAF on December 17, 1993, 90 years to the day after the Wright brothers' success at Kittyhawk.

The B-2 was originally conceived as a strategic penetrator, capable of passing untouched through the Soviet Union's most sophisticated defenses to drop nuclear weapons. Armed with up to 40,000 pounds of conventional munitions, the B-2 uses its GPS Aided Targeting System (GATS) in combination with weapons such as the Joint Direct Attack Munition (JDAM), and has its APQ-181 radar to help in aiming bombs fitted with a GPS-aided "smart" guidance tail kit. Sixteen targets can be attacked in a single pass. The blending of low-observable technologies with high aerodynamic efficiency gives the B-2 significant advantages over previous bombers. Composite materials, special coatings and the shaped flying-wing design reduce the B-2's infrared, acoustic, electromagnetic, visual and radar signatures, and these stealthy characteristics offer greater freedom for the bomber to operate at high altitude, where the sensors get a better field of view and the range without refueling is some 6,000 nautical miles — or

more than 10,000 nms with just one refueling. This tremendous capability means that the B-2 could be tasked to fly anywhere in the world to deliver a variety of weapons in less than 24 hours. All this sophistication comes at a considerable price, quoted by the U.S. Air Force as $1.157 billion per aircraft in 1998 dollars. However, responsibility for flying the B-2 is shared by a crew of only two, a pilot in the left seat and mission commander in the right, compared to the B-1B's four and the B-52's five.

Twenty-one B-2s were built and are operated by the 509th Bomb Wing at Whiteman Air Force Base, Missouri. Whiteman was the B-2's only operational base until early 2003, when facilities for the B-2 were built on the British island of Diego Garcia in the Indian Ocean, followed by deployment to Guam in 2005. One criticism of the B-2 was that it too expensive to risk in combat. However, the aircraft has so far seen service in three campaigns. Its operational debut was during the Kosovo War in 1999, and since then the aircraft has been tasked with operating over Afghanistan in Operation Enduring Freedom and Iraq in Operation Iraqi Freedom. Some missions to Iraq were flown from Whiteman AFB and were the longest ever attempted, one mission lasting over 50 hours. This was possible because the B-2 is highly automated, and one crewmember can sleep, use a flush toilet or prepare a hot meal while the other monitors the aircraft's systems. Jack Northrop may have been surprised if he could have seen the B-2, but he would assuredly have approved.

A B-2 Spirit from the 13th Expeditionary Bomb Squadron departs on a training mission during one of the final sorties of a four-month deployment to Andersen Air Force Base, Guam, August 24, 2006.

F-35 Lightning II

Joint Strike Fighter

THE F-35 REPRESENTS A MAJOR advance in military aviation. It is an aircraft for the 21st century and as such is being developed as a highly integrated air-combat system, the key parts of which are the stealthy airframe, the propulsion elements, the weapons systems, the avionics suite, and an autonomic logistics system.

Three versions of the F-35 will be produced — a conventional takeoff-and-landing variant (CTOL) for the U.S. Air Force, a navalized version (CV) for the U.S. Navy, and a short-takeoff/vertical landing version (STOVL) for the U.S. Marine Corps and for Britain's Royal Air Force and Royal Navy. The requirements for the multirole F-35 are therefore complex. Military aviators want it to be uncompromisingly lethal, while still being affordable. It must be able to survive the challenges of 21st-century combat and be supportable when operating from austere environments anywhere in the world. At the same time, the F-35 must meet all of the diverse needs of its various customers.

In October 2001, an international team led by Lockheed Martin was awarded the contract to build the Joint Strike Fighter. Twenty-two aircraft were to be built for the programs System Development and Demonstration (SDD) phase — 14 for test flying and eight more for ground testing. Lockheed Martin (F-22 and stealth experience) leads a team that includes Northrop Grumman (stealth technology and carrier operations), and BAE Systems (short takeoff and vertical landing experience). Early production lots of all three F-35 variants will be powered by the Pratt and Whitney afterburning turbofan F-135 engine. Later production aircraft could use either the F135 or the F-136 turbofan being developed by General Electric and Rolls-Royce. On the

The United States Marines, the RAF and the Royal Navy will fly the F-35B STOVL (Short Take-Off and Vertical Landing) version, seen here hovering with lift fan doors open. **Opposite:** The future of aerial supremacy, the Lockheed F-35 banks into the rising sun. The F-35 is an evolution of the Joint Strike Fighter program developed by the Department of Defense in the search for the next generation multiuse aircraft. Lockheed Martin is the winner of the competition to build the JSF.

F-35B, the engine is coupled with a shaft-driven lift fan system developed by Rolls-Royce which can generate more than 20,000 pounds of thrust. Doors on the top and bottom of the fuselage open as the vertical fan spins up to provide vertical lift. Nine nations are partnering in the F-35's SDD phase: the United States, the United Kingdom, Italy, the Netherlands, Turkey, Canada, Denmark, Norway and Australia.

The F-35A is the standard variant being developed for the biggest customer, the USAF, to replace the F-16 and the A-10. It will probably also be the most exported variant, possibly to current F-16, F-4 and F/A-18 operators, such as the Netherlands, Belgium, Denmark, Norway, Turkey, Greece, Israel and Australia.

To minimise the F-35's radar signature, the sweep angles are identical for the leading and trailing edges of the wing and tailplane; the fuselage and canopy have sloping sides; the canopy seam and the weapon bay doors are sawtoothed; and the fins are canted at an angle. The USMC F-35B is similar in outline to the F-35A, but with a slightly shorter range because some of the fuselage fuel tank space is used for the lift fan. The F-35C's structure and landing gear have been strengthened to cope with catapult launches and arrested landings. It has a greater wing area than other variants and larger control surfaces for better low speed handling. The F-35C will complement the U.S. Navy's fleet of F/A-18E/F fighters, replacing F/A-18 A/Cs.

Weapons are loaded internally in two parallel bays in front of the landing gear. Each weapons bay is fitted with two hardpoints for carrying a range of bombs and missiles. Weapons to be cleared for internal carriage include JDAM (Joint Direct Attack Munition),

CBU-105 WCMD (Wind-Corrected Munitions Dispenser) for the Sensor-Fuzed Weapon, JSOW (Joint StandOff Weapon), Paveway II guided bombs, AIM-120C AMRAAM air-to-air missile. For external carriage: JASSM (Joint Air-to-Surface Standoff Missile), AIM-9X Sidewinder and Storm Shadow cruise missile. The USAF F-35 has an internally mounted gun, and other variants can have an external gun pod fitted.

In-service dates are likely to be 2012 for the USMC, 2013 for the USAF, 2014 for the U.S. Navy and the U.K. services. More than 2,500 F-35s are expected to be bought by the U.S. and U.K., and the potential for export to other countries is good, perhaps raising total production to 5,000 or more. Lockheed Martin in Fort Worth, Texas, will manufacture the F-35's forward fuselage and wings, and will also be responsible for final assembly of the

The F-35 AA-1, in the flight line hangar at Lockheed/Martin's assembly facility in Fort Worth, Texas. The first flights of this initial USAF fighter were made in December of 2006. The next fighter to come down the production line will be the F-35 BA-1. The designations mean A for Air Force and B for U.S. Marine Corps and the U.K. Royal Air Force and Royal Navy.

Jon Beesely, Lockheed Martin's chief test pilot, is the only man in the world to have flown the F-35. Beesely also test-flew the F-22 Raptor and was one of the first pilots to fly the F-117 Nighthawk. This soft-spoken man is the latest in a long line of talented aviators who have flown for Lockheed Martin.

aircraft. Northrop Grumman will manufacture the center fuselage in Palmdale and El Segundo, California, and the aft fuselage and tail unit will be built by BAE Systems in Samlesbury, England. Flight-testing will be conducted at Fort Worth, Edwards Air Force Base, and Naval Air Station Patuxent River. Additionally, the STOVL and CV variants will undergo sea trials aboard American, British and Italian aircraft carriers.

Some idea of the vast array of companies involved in the F-35 program can be gauged from the following partial list: electro-optical targeting system, Lockheed Martin; thermal imaging system, Northrop Grumman; lasers, BAE Systems; multifunction radar, Northrop Grumman; integrated electronic warfare suite, BAE Systems; side stick and throttle controls, BAE Systems; helmet-mounted display, Vision Systems International (a partnership between Kaiser Electronics and Elbit of Israel); antenna suite, Ball Aerospace; advanced avionics systems, infrastructure, image processing, digital map software, fibre optics, high-speed communications links, Harris Corporation; radar altimeter, inertial navigation/global positioning system and air data transducers, Honeywell; 24-channel GPS with digital anti-jam receiver,

Raytheon; upper wing skins, ATK Composites; lower wing skins, Vought Aircraft Industries; electronic control systems, electrical power system (with Hamilton Sundstrand), integrated canopy frame, Smiths Aerospace; wheels and brakes, Honeywell; fuel system, hydraulics for lift fan, engine controls and accessories, Parker Aerospace; primary flight control Electrohydrostatic Actuation System, leading edge flap drive system and wing-fold system, Moog Inc; pneumatic weapon delivery system, EDO Corporation; lift-fan anti-icing system, Goodrich; electrical wiring, Stork Aerospace.

All of this testifies to the complexity of the process of building a combat aircraft for the 21st century. The planning and organization required are prodigious, but they will produce a machine that could be in service for forty years. By that time, manned combat aircraft may well have been overtaken by events. The progress in developing unmanned aerial vehicles is already so rapid that some pilots, like those who control Global Hawk, have exchanged the cockpit for an armchair. In the F-35 we may be seeing the last hurrah of fighter pilots in the tradition of Ball and Richthofen, Bader and Hartmann, Bong and Sakai.

Photographer's Acknowledgments

This overview of 50 great aircraft includes the visual work of some of our colleagues who also strive to create quality images, in artwork and in photographs. We acknowledge their contributions. Gil Cohen, Paul Rendel, Michael Turner, Bill Marsalko and Mariusz Adamski are some of the best in the world. The Museum of Flight in Seattle, Washington, has an archive that is unsurpassed in depth and quality, and the same must be said for photo archivist Katherine Williams. The Special Collections and Archives at Wright State University and Dawne Dewey have also been of invaluable help. The photo archives at Lockheed/Martin and Denny Lombard always come through with just the right images. Thanks to Fred Hotson for his archival image of the DHC Beaver. Nearly all of the archival images in this book are drawn from the *Aviation Century* series and our acknowledgments are noted in each of the five volumes.

Thanks also to PageWave Graphics, led by Andrew Smith and Joseph Gisini — we have developed a wonderful working friendship that has made the pages of these books a pleasure to look at, over and over.

Our editor, Kathy Fraser, has put up with a lot. Discussions about the finer points of the English language, and how they apply to aviation, are always lively. The use of the word "aeroplane," for instance — as opposed to aircraft, airplane or plane — is just one of many areas of debate and inquiry that have expanded our knowledge of a subject we thought we knew.

Finally, I must thank my partner, Ron Dick. I cannot recall anyone else who has squeezed more out of life than Ron. He's facing a great challenge now and the previously clearly defined road is more than a bit out of focus. I've read a lot about aviation, and for the past fourteen years, a lot of Ron's text (500,000 words just for this project), and there isn't a better man to tell a story about flying, including all the facts, with just enough technical information to make the case, and still give us the sense of being above the earth, the sun glinting off the wingtips, flying into the deep blue sky.

Bibliographical Note from the Editor

This book and the *Aviation Century* series that preceded it are the result of a couple of lifetimes spent acquiring knowledge through much research, countless conversations, thousands of miles of travel, truckloads of film, paper and ink and, above all, many unforgettable personal experiences. The list of written resources consulted or in some way contributing to the creation of this particular volume is too long to include in this short space. For a more complete listing of sources and suggested readings, please see the bibliographies of any or all of the five volumes of the *Aviation Century* series. If you wish to prolong your enjoyment of this book and discover more about the ways in which aviation has changed the world, look no further than those five volumes by Ron Dick and Dan Patterson: *Aviation Century: The Early Years*; *The Golden Age*; *World War II*; *Wings of Change*; and *War & Peace in the Air*.

Index